SAY ALL THE
UNSPOKEN
THINGS

SAY ALL THE
UNSPOKEN
THINGS

A BOOK
of
LETTERS

JOHN SOWERS

W PUBLISHING GROUP

AN IMPRINT OF THOMAS NELSON

Published in Nashville, Tennessee, by W Publishing, an imprint of Thomas Nelson.

Thomas Nelson titles may be purchased in bulk for educational, business, fundraising, or sales promotional use. For information, please email SpecialMarkets@ThomasNelson.com.

Unless otherwise noted, Scripture quotations are taken from the Holy Bible, New International Version®, NIV®. Copyright © 1973, 1978, 1984, 2011 by Biblica, Inc.® Used by permission of Zondervan. All rights reserved worldwide. www.zondervan.com. The "NIV" and "New International Version" are trademarks registered in the United States Patent and Trademark Office by Biblica, Inc.®

Scripture quotations marked ESV are taken from the ESV® Bible (The Holy Bible, English Standard Version®). Copyright © 2001 by Crossway, a publishing ministry of Good News Publishers. Used by permission. All rights reserved.

Scripture quotations marked MSG are taken from THE MESSAGE. Copyright © 1993, 2002, 2018 by Eugene H. Peterson. Used by permission of NavPress. All rights reserved. Represented by Tyndale House Publishers, a Division of Tyndale House Ministries.

Scripture quotations marked NLT are taken from the Holy Bible, New Living Translation. Copyright © 1996, 2004, 2015 by Tyndale House Foundation. Used by permission of Tyndale House Ministries, Carol Stream, Illinois 60188. All rights reserved.

Any internet addresses, phone numbers, or company or product information printed in this book are offered as a resource and are not intended in any way to be or to imply an endorsement by Thomas Nelson, nor does Thomas Nelson vouch for the existence, content, or services of these sites, phone numbers, companies, or products beyond the life of this book.

ISBN 978-0-7852-4077-8 (audiobook)
ISBN 978-0-7852-4076-1 (eBook)
ISBN 978-0-7852-4075-4 (TP)

Library of Congress Control Number: 2021947718

Printed in the United States of America

22 23 24 25 26   LSC   10 9 8 7 6 5 4 3 2 1

for Rosie, Dass, and Evangeline

You taught me the courage of stars before you left
How light carries on endlessly, even after death
With shortness of breath
You explained the infinite
How rare and beautiful it is to even exist

—FROM "SATURN" BY SLEEPING AT LAST

CONTENTS

CONTENTS

AUTHOR'S NOTE

I began writing these letters to my daughters in early 2020—one year after I lost my mom, their nana. I felt empty knowing there were no more conversations with her. No more stories or laughs or wise insights. She was gone.

Death has implications. There is urgency to it. When the end is near, either our own or that of a loved one, we may feel a rush of urgency. Have we done all we need to do? Have we forgiven? Have we thanked them? Have we told them we love them? Have we poured out our full, beating hearts to them?

I started writing these letters to speak my full heart to my daughters, to tell them I love them and pass on everything given to me. Just after I began writing, the COVID-19 pandemic reached the United States. Within months, everyone was wearing masks and staying inside, not wanting to catch or transmit the virus. Millions got sick, and, as of this writing, over three million people worldwide have died, and the numbers continue to increase. Many lost jobs and suffered financial and psychological hardships. My girls did virtual school. I wrote this book locked away in my cabin.

Every day, we heard voices telling us about infection rates, death counts, and why we should stay home and act responsibly. The year was filled with loss as death brushed its cold fingers across our cheeks. We were all reminded that every day might be our last. I wrote these letters with these things in mind. And with our shared experience of 2020, maybe they have something for all of us.

THE UNSPOKEN THINGS

January 3, 2020

Dear Rosie, Dass, and Evangeline,

I remember standing over Nana's bed.

She was sleeping on her back, head looking left. I touched her socked toe and whispered, "Mom, Mom." She opened one eye, looked at me, and then went back to sleep. I decided it was best to let her sleep. That was the last time I saw her alive.

A month earlier, you girls decorated her house on Christmas Eve, surprising her when she came home from the hospital. She smiled that whole night. I'm glad you were with her on her last Christmas; you always made her so happy. Nana loved you more than you know.

Weeks before she passed, a friend from Atlanta called me and said something powerful: "Tell her you love her, and say all the unspoken things." I did. I told her I loved her and thanked her for being so good to us.

And those were the words I said at her funeral: *Say all the unspoken things.*

Many of us go through life with words and feelings stranded in our hearts. Words we deeply feel but never say. Sometimes we never have the chance. We don't always get to say goodbye. We don't always know when will be our last hug, high five, smile, laugh, or "I love you."

All we have is today, now, and what we do in this one shining moment.

When we speak with someone for the last time, sometimes the magic happens. Sometimes our hearts unlock stranded words, words hidden away for years. Deep words. Forgiving words. Sometimes grace finds us, and we speak our full hearts and all those good things we feel for another person.

These moments are rare. I'm not sure why we hold back and live in the shallows. Maybe fear keeps us from wading out. Maybe we're afraid we will be embarrassed or our love won't be returned. Maybe it goes back to Adam and Eve, who fell from grace and were ashamed and made clothes to cover themselves, hiding from each other and God. Maybe we're just good at hiding too.

I think children are better than adults at being honest. Children say and do what they feel. They smile and shout and red-faced scream and hug and throw themselves on the ground. I love when you girls shriek, run, and jump on me, saying, "I love you, Daddy!" Then I pick you up and wrap you in my arms like a giant burrito. I love these moments. And I know, in a few years, there probably won't be as much shrieking and jumping.

I don't want to leave any words stranded in my heart. This is why I'm writing to you now. I hope these letters grow with you as you grow. Maybe they can help you find your way, or if you feel stuck or uncertain, maybe one of them will unlock something for you. I hope you pass them down to your children and their children.

My grandmother Helen wrote me a letter once a week, for many years, on Monet cards. Her letters always said how much she loved me and was praying for me. My great-grandfather wrote dozens of love letters to his wife, Nettie. I still have those letters. On the day Nana was born, Nettie wrote her a letter saying, "Welcome to the family."

Nana worked three jobs to provide for me and your uncle Bill, so she didn't write many letters. But her life was a beautiful letter, the way she gave and lived and loved us.

Our lives are letters to those around us. I hope my life is a love letter to you.

I hope you know how much I love you.

I hope these letters have the same magic as those last conversations with Nana. I hope they make you smile and laugh. I hope they pass along the love and wisdom given to me. I hope they say all the unspoken things. And when you read them, know that I am loving you even if we are separated by many miles and years.

All my love forever,
Dad

PART 1

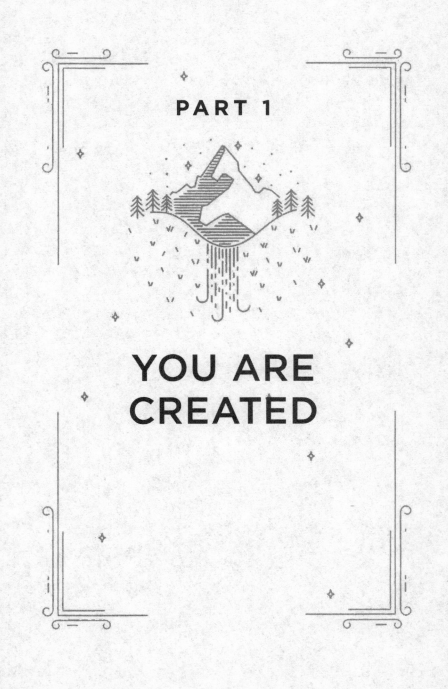

YOU ARE CREATED

CHAPTER 1

CREATED

February 10, 2020

Dear Rosie, Dass, and Evangeline,

I remember the nights you girls came into the world.

Rosie, you had raven-black hair and compassion on your brow. Bright and full of spirit and movement. You still like to move. Dass, you came next. Flapping your arms and crying softly. Your cries sounded just like a little bird singing. You still like to sing. Eva, you came along a few years later, full of stardust, smiles, and shiny goodness. You still like to shine. Three immortal souls, leaving your homes in the womb and entering the world, drawing your first tender breaths.

I remember watching your tiny chests rise and fall, listening to you breathe. Holding you for the first time felt beautiful and magical. My hands were filled with the radiant treasure of you, and I was stunned by glory.

Since then, I've loved watching the three of you grow. Singing "Amazing Grace" as you fall asleep on my forearm. Watching you crawl and take your first wobbly steps. Telling bedtime stories with you as the main characters. Pushing you on the tree swing; pulling you in the wagon. Celebrating your first bike rides in the church parking lot, first back handsprings, first basketball and soccer goals. Receiving your art from school. *To Dad, Love Rosie, Dass, Eva.* Nothing prepared me for the love and joy I found in you. Nothing.

But long before I loved you, long before I knew your faces, before you were born, before the earth was made, before the oceans rolled and the sun blazed in the sky, and any star was spoken into existence, God knew you and loved you. This reminds me of a song, Psalm 139:

> You created my inmost being;
> > you knit me together in my mother's
> > > womb. . . .
> My frame was not hidden from you
> > when I was made in the secret place,
> > when I was woven together in the depths of
> > > the earth.
> Your eyes saw my unformed body;
> > all the days ordained for me were written in
> > > your book
> > before one of them came to be.

I've only known you a few years, but God has known you since before the creation of the world, before time began. When God spoke everything into being, when he created light, the sun, the moon and stars, the earth and oceans, trees, animals, birds, and fish, he thought of you. When he created time, space, matter, power, and motion, he thought of you. He thinks of you more than all the sand on the seashore, which means he is always thinking of you.

He created you and knows everything about you. Every hair on your heads. Your voice and unique fingerprints. The flecks of color in your eyes. He knitted you together in your mother's womb and watches your every step. He created you, calls you, and loves you more than anything I can describe or write in a book.

There will be many voices in your lives calling you. These voices will tell you who you are, what you should believe, what you need to buy, how you should spend your time. You will hear voices from friends and strangers and schoolmates, from televisions and internet ads and online forums and social media. But over all the clatter and the noise, I pray you remember and claim this truth for yourselves—*you are created*.

He thought of you. He chose you. He loves you. He wants you to be here.

This is the deepest truth of your lives: [You were] created through him and for him. You were formed in the eternal well of love, made for relationship with him and one another. And this truth answers our deepest questions: *Who am I? Why am I here? What is my purpose?*

I want to tell you so many things. And I feel small when writing them. Who am I to write about infinite mysteries? Or infinite thoughts before the creation of the world? I am still learning and don't have all the answers. Sometimes when we think we have all the answers, we are actually a great distance from them. I think some of these mysteries are knowable, at least in part.

I am not the best representative of these things. Maybe someone like Pastor John or Aunt Julie would be a better person to write these letters to you. I've been an imperfect example; I've made mistakes and will make more. I hope you can learn wisdom from my mistakes. I'm sorry for my failings and for the times I have hurt you. All I can do is ask forgiveness, change, and trust the grace of God to cover it all.

Years ago, I worked in a church with young people, with children in junior high and high school. I still talk to some of them. There were three girls in the group, sisters. Their dad, Mark, was a kind man, full of joy. Always smiling. A leader in church and served with me in the homeless shelter. Sometimes he sang onstage.

Then one day, we found out Mark had cancer and was dying.

A couple of months later, everyone was standing around his hospital bed. It happened so fast. He was so young and alive. Then, everyone was holding his hand, telling him they loved him. The heart monitor flatlined. It was over. But then Mark opened his eyes! He was smiling. Mark was back, but only for a moment. His face was shining, full of light, and he kept saying, "Beautiful. Beautiful. It's so beautiful."

His wife asked, "What? What do you see?"

Mark smiled and whispered, "Things too wonderful to tell."

God is infinite and intimate, hidden and revealed, mysterious and clear.

And some things are too wonderful to tell.

You were created,
Dad

CHAPTER 2

WITH

February 15, 2020

Dear Rosie, Dass, and Evangeline,

Evangeline, you are asleep now. Your head is resting on my shoulder, your little curls in a wild tangle. It's a magical thing when you fall asleep on me. It's like I am your security blanket, and you make me your human pillow. And I had your same curls. My grandmother told Nana, "Don't cut them or they won't grow back."

Nana worked hard. She worked three jobs to provide for me and your uncle Bill. She often came home late, so we went out to eat most nights. She liked Franke's. Baked fish. Turnip greens. Carrots. She always asked about my day, my life, school, and sports, and she sat quietly and listened well.

My grandmother Helen moved from the country to the city to help raise us. She picked me up from school every day, her blue Mercury always first in line. She always smiled at me. And she had snacks or drinks, and she'd say something kind, like, "You're such a right handsome young man; I love how you walk tall. You make me so proud." She was always proud.

Back then, my secret plan was to play baseball for the Red Sox. So I practiced hard after school every day and on weekends. Nana knew about my dream and took me to baseball games. In the summers, she took me to Dallas to watch the Red Sox play the Rangers. The Red Sox were not her team; they were my team. She never played baseball, but she cheered for them with me. She loved the things I loved because she loved me. I think love does that.

My grandmother built her life around me too. Before she moved to the city, she drove me to her house on weekends where we spent the night. We went to an old country store, Cotham's. She bought me cupcakes. We went to her little church. She had a cat. A black one named Midnight. Like your cat, Shadow.

My grandmother taught me to read and write and draw straight lines. And I loved drawing, so she took me to art classes. I loved movies, so she took me to see *Star Wars*.

Whenever she came in the house she always said, "Woo-hoo" in this sing-songy voice, letting us know it was her. When I was sick, Mom had to work, so Grandmother stayed with me. I laid on the couch, and she made sure I had everything I needed. She cared for me and nursed me back to health.

She found ways to show up for me, even after I moved away for college. Every week, she wrote me letters saying how much she loved me, was praying for me, and was proud of me. She was always there for me. She showed up.

Those who mean the most to us are those who show up in our lives.

My friend Ed is good at this too. I met him about ten years ago in Portland. Ed is a great husband and dad. He's one of the best guitar players in the world. When life got hard, I called Ed. He didn't offer advice or try to change or edit my thoughts. He just listened quietly and calmly. Then he started checking on me. He called or texted once a day for the next few years. He answered every time I called; it didn't matter if he was walking onstage or eating dinner with family. Ed showed up.

When someone shows up for you, it's like having a strong anchor. You can't see them, but you know they are there, holding and tethering you to something deep and solid. Keeping you steady when it feels like your life will capsize. When someone faithfully shows up for you, it is a silent and powerful reminder: *I have someone. I am not alone.*

I called Ed the morning Nana died.

He wanted to come check on me; I told him not to worry about it. But he came anyway. Got in his Jeep and drove five hours through the rainy night and told me, "You don't need to be alone."

Ed stayed a week and helped me make the hard decisions. When someone dies, you talk to doctors and nurses, call the funeral home, get death certificates. There are a million dreary things to do when you don't feel like doing any of them. Ed helped with all of it. And before he left, he asked me if he needed to stay longer.

Showing up means we are with someone, no matter what. We walk with them through darkness, believing the best for them. We accept them. We don't judge. We just show up. Like Nana. Like Ed. Like my grandmother. Showing up for someone is a way to say "I love you" without words. Showing up for someone says, "I am here for you."

When I was young, on Christmas Eve, my grandmother would drive me to the country and take me to her little church. Sometimes it was icy, and she held my forearm as we walked inside. We lit candles and sang "Silent Night," and I learned how God came into our world just like you girls, as a sweet baby. Wrapped and swaddled just like you. Maybe he fell asleep on his dad's shoulder. Maybe his cries sounded like a little bird too.

The Bible says his name is Immanuel, which means "God is with us." He shows up. This is our great promise. He is always with us, even when life is overwhelming and too much. Even if we feel alone. Even if we lose ourselves and forget who we are. He loves us, he accepts us, and he shows up in our losses and wins, in our disasters and magnificent defeats.

Jesus is the Son who is with us.

Every Christmas morning, I called Grandmother to come over so we could open presents. I still remember her phone number. I wasn't allowed to call her until seven. She drove over and brought a brown grocery bag filled with presents and sat in her chair. I still have that chair. She sat there, smiling and watching us and saying, "Ooh, thank you" whenever she opened a present. I can still hear her voice saying, "Thank you. Love you, honey."

She was always there for me, a quiet, kind presence. I think God shows up in our lives like this. He doesn't force himself on us. He's not loud. His voice is powerful; he created the universe by speaking it into being. But he is humble, and he is with us.

And I don't think he likes to raise his voice. I think he would rather whisper.

He is with you,
Dad

CHAPTER 3
DAD

March 10, 2020

Dear Rosie, Dass, and Evangeline,

Today, Evangeline, you ran to me and started jumping up and down, up and down, like you were on some invisible, happy trampoline. Belly laughing and saying, "Daddy." Then you hugged my leg and said, "Up top!" So I picked you up and put you on my shoulders. Then we went on a hike.

Whenever I come to school for lunch, you big girls want me to sit between you. I don't eat much because I'm just happy to be with you and to watch you. And you don't know it yet, but I'm building you a secret treehouse.

It won't be a surprise by the time you read this. I hope you climb and play in it, paint and laugh, read books and have dance parties. I hope you dream big dreams. I hope you write great stories. I hope you train as athletes, writers, and anything else you want to do and be. I thought about you as I designed it. Every day I work on it, I think of you. And I can't wait for you to see it. I hope you love it and it makes you smile.

When you smile, your eyes flicker like candles. Smiles are sometimes a way to say "I love you." I love picking you up after school. You smile at me, and sometimes you bring me drawings that I hang up at the cabin. Gifts are another way to say "I love you."

Rosie, you often say, "You are the second-best dad ever. God is the best; you are second." Dad is my favorite name. When I was younger, I didn't like the word *Dad*. I never said it. Not *Dad* or *Father* or *Daddy*. But you girls changed all that. Now Dad is my favorite name. And I know I cannot claim second place, but you are right about the first. God is the best dad. But you call me second best because that's what love does. Love speaks life and hope.

Love sees the best in us and believes.

This reminds me of a story of a dad who had two sons. One day, the younger son said, "Dad, give me all the money coming to me when you die."

Even though it was a greedy request, the father divided the property between his sons. The younger son quickly packed his bags and left home. The father stood in the doorway and watched. Soon after the son arrived in the new city, he went out and bought fancy clothes, food, and drinks. He gambled with his new money and stayed up all night acting wild and reckless. He was the life of the party. A quiet voice in his heart warned him, repeatedly telling him to stop, but he ignored it.

He lived like this for several weeks, until his debit card was rejected. He was out of money. He went back to his fancy hotel room, but his key didn't work anymore. All his new friends were gone. He didn't have anywhere to go. He was thirsty and found a public bathroom. Maybe he could drink from the sink. As he drank, he looked in the mirror. His bloodshot eyes were sunken and tired, and his face was covered in shadow.

He had nothing to eat. He was broke, hungry, exhausted.

Then the economy crashed, and the whole country was broke. Food was hard to find. Restaurants and grocery stores closed. So he started sleeping outside. Anywhere he could find shelter, in boxes, under cars or bridges. Sometimes, if he was lucky, he would find an unlocked car and sleep inside. He dug through trash cans to find food. He made a cardboard sign and stood on street corners: *Hungry. Need Food. Please Help.*

But no one gave him any. Sometimes he talked to himself just to hear a voice. It made him feel less alone. But the worst part, the worst part was the shame. Shame hung around his neck like a heavy weight, making him feel like a failure. He thought he had wasted his life, his father's gift, his health, his money, everything. He felt lifeless and alone. He felt so far from home.

Then one day, he had an idea. He realized the people who worked for his dad ate three meals a day, while he was out here, broke and starving. *Life is better at home*, he thought. "Life is better at home," he said out loud. Just saying the word *home* made him feel lighter and gave him strength. So he made a plan. The son decided to beg his father for forgiveness, to apologize and say, "Father, I've sinned against heaven and against you, and I am not worthy to be called your son. Please hire me back as a worker." He was so ashamed, he didn't even feel worthy to be a son anymore.

Then he got up and limped home to his father.

While the son was still a long way off, his father saw him and ran to him. He grabbed his son, hugged him, and held on to him for a long time. The son started into his apology, but the father was not listening. You see, the father had already forgiven his son. The father had stayed up many nights, hoping and praying for his son to return. Now he was just happy his son was home.

The father shouted to his workers, "Bring me a clean set of clothes and the family ring! Let's throw a party! My son is home! My son is home! For he was lost and now is found!"

And the father could not stop smiling.

God is the Father who loves us.

No matter what we've done, no matter how far we run, God loves us, waits for us, and wants us home. Even when we feel like we must work our way back to him. Even if we feel like we don't deserve to be his children anymore. Our Father runs to us, hugs us, throws us a party, and says, "Everything I own is yours."

This story has shaped much of my thinking about God.

Sometimes when people talk about God, they think of religious things. Sometimes people use God's name to influence politics or control people. But I'm not talking about politics or religious things, which sometimes feel like duty, responsibility, moralism, punishments, and all those things we should do.

I am not talking about anything we do. I am talking about the Father who loves us, waits for us, runs to us, and never gives up on us. Our relationship with him starts with our response to his love. It begins when we say yes to his invitation and then yes again, every day, for the rest of our lives.

Many people feel like the younger brother. Our poor decisions, bad experiences, and failures expose us to shame. We feel unacceptable, like we don't belong. Shame tries to keep us away from the Father's house. Or it makes us believe we must earn our way back. Shame is one of the most powerful and corrosive forces in the world.

"I am no longer worthy to be called your son."

To me, this is the saddest line in the story. The lost son felt like he was out of the family. He felt like he had to earn his way back, but as a servant, not a son. He didn't believe he was even worthy to be a son anymore. He thought his father's love had changed, and he was no longer welcome.

But the father would have none of it.

At different times in my life, I have acted like the lost son, trying to fill my heart with substitutes. As Henri Nouwen said, "I am the prodigal son every time I search for unconditional love where it cannot be found." I pursued fame through writing. Speaking. Baseball. Social media. Relationships. Sometimes I loved these things more than I loved my Father's house. I chased them and filled my life with them. None of them satisfied me. And the tighter I clung to them, the emptier and colder I became.

I never meant to walk away. But I did. I packed my bags, left the Father's house, and took up residence in the distant country. God became like a friend I once knew and still loved but lost touch with somewhere along the way. I missed him but accepted the distance as normal. I'm the one who walked away. Just like the lost son, I felt cold and sad. I was homesick. Over time, I forgot the heart of the Father.

But love sees the best in us and believes.

Even when it is our fault. Even when we have blown it. Even when we don't feel good enough. The whole time we are gone, he misses and waits for us. He is the Waiting Father. It is grace for us to wake up and come to our senses. Grace to remember. Grace to feel homesick. Grace to stand up and limp back home.

My spiritual walk is marked by returns and reunions. Much of my spiritual life can be described by what Brennan Manning called "the victorious limp."

When we finally limp home, our Father runs to meet us.

There is no stern lecture. No "I told you so." No shame or silent treatment. God doesn't demand us to clean up before we come home. He accepts us just as we are. We don't have to act a certain way or dress fancy to be welcome. He showers us with gifts and throws a party for us. He reminds us who we are, and he cheers and celebrates us. More than anything, he's just happy we're home.

You are always welcome home,
Dad

CHAPTER 4

HOME

March 18, 2020

Dear Rosie, Dass, and Evangeline,

There's a second part to the story of the Waiting Father, and here it is.

While the party for the lost son was happening inside, the older brother was outside working in the field. When he came home, he could hear music, smell the steak, and see the party. "What in the world is going on?" he asked.

A worker replied, "Your brother came home, and your father is having a party for him!"

But instead of being happy his brother was home, the older brother was outraged. He threw down his garden tools and stayed outside, away from the party and his brother.

After a while, the father came outside and invited him in: "What's wrong? Why don't you come in and enjoy the party with us?"

But the older brother huffed, "I've always been good. I never ran away from home. I didn't waste your money. But you've never thrown a party for me! He doesn't belong here! He doesn't deserve any of this!"

The father replied in a soft voice, "My son, you don't understand. You are my son, and everything I have is yours. It has always been yours. But your brother is home now. We must celebrate. For your brother was dead, and now he's alive; he was lost, and now he is found."

The older brother was upset. He thought the father's love was based on what he and his brother did: *He did this, so he deserves that. I did this, so I deserve that.*

What if the older brother had met his younger brother at the door instead of the father? Would he have hugged his brother and welcomed him home? Would he have thrown a party? Would he have even let him in? No. My guess is he would have acted toward his brother exactly as he did toward his father. Angry and upset and red-faced. With clenched teeth and fists, hissing, "I can't believe what you did. You blew it. You don't belong here. Get out!" Maybe he would have slammed the door in his face.

The first few times I read this story, I was shocked and sad about how the younger son acted, and I was heartbroken when he threw everything away. The story seemed like a contrast between the younger son's bad decisions and the grace of the Waiting Father who wanted his son home. When the son came home, the father ignored his excuses and welcomed him back. I used to think this story was about the younger son and the father's response. Now I know the older brother was lost too. The younger brother ran away from home and lost himself. The older brother stayed at home but was lost in judgment. And the father loved them both.

I have been the younger brother who walked away from home.

I have been the older brother who lived in shame and judgment.

I have wrongfully judged people and tried to be a gatekeeper for the Father's house: *This person belongs. That person does not.* But the voice of the older brother in me is not usually aimed at others; it is aimed at myself. I am mostly accepting and forgiving of others, but not as accepting and forgiving of myself. Shame tells me that I don't belong, that I must earn my way back home.

For many years, I believed the Father was like the older brother. I imagined God to have a stern face and crossed arms. He stood over me, frowning. Whenever I failed, he was disappointed. This was true when I got divorced. I felt like I didn't deserve my room in the Father's house anymore. I believed my place was based on my performance. It was something I earned through my own efforts. And I no longer deserved my room.

I believed that when I was good, God was happy. And when I failed, I thought he would kick me out. I lived in fear. When I finally did fail, I felt like God (or at least the god I imagined) was giving me an eviction notice. *Get out.*

This idea kept my heart away from God for several years. I missed him but didn't think I belonged anymore. I thought God was upset with me, so how could I ever return? I thought, *Maybe someday I will try to work my way back home like the younger brother did, but not today. Not today.* I felt like an exile. And I didn't realize this until I talked about it with my friend Ben. He said, "You have forgotten the heart of the Father."

He said, "What if one of your daughters came to you crying and hurt? Would you stand over her with a stern face and crossed arms telling her to get it together? Would you tell her she was no longer welcome? No. Of course not. You would scoop her up, take her home, and love her. Even if she messed up, you would love her without flinching. That is your heart. And that is the heart of the Father."

Sometimes the story we tell ourselves, the story we believe and repeat in our own minds, is the story of the older brother. We believe the lies of shame and judgment. We rehearse our failures over and over again, and keep reliving the guilt we feel from them. Rejection and shame become our self-made prison.

Shame misses the whole point of grace. Grace is a free, undeserved gift. It's not something we work for or earn or something we can repay or even need to try to repay. Some people think, *You gave me this, so I must give you something in return.* That is not grace; it is a gift exchange. Grace requires no gift back, no payment. We just receive it freely and with open hands.

Here's the news: None of us deserves a room in the Father's house. Not the one the world says is a failure; not the one who acts like a dutiful and religious son. This is the beauty of grace. Because of Jesus, we are all welcome. And he says, "My Father's house has many rooms; . . . I am going there to prepare a place for you."

We are all invited to the feast.

> You always have a place,
> Dad

If you don't make the soccer team
or fall off the balance beam,
if you fail your math grades
or mess up in the band parade,
I love you just the same.
If you stand outside in the cold,
and life didn't work out as you prayed,
if you feel alone and lonely,

and all your friends have gone away,
I love you just the same.
If you lose your money, your dream,
and even forget your name,
if you look up one day with sad eyes
and feel far, far away, remember,
I love you just the same.

PART 2

IDENTITY
AND
PURPOSE

CHAPTER 5

LIFE

April 12, 2020 (Easter Sunday)

Dear Rosie, Dass, and Evangeline,

I remember seeing my grandmother just after she passed.

All these memories came for me. They came fast, moving and spinning like a kaleidoscope. They came unbidden; I didn't have to reach for them. I don't know what called them to the surface. They just came. Maybe love called them. Maybe love brings us memories and floods us with appreciation as our hearts prepare to say goodbye.

My grandmother slept in a shower cap to protect her fancy hair. I don't think women do that anymore. Maybe they do; what do I know? One time, when I was a young boy, I wanted to wear a shower cap too. So I did. And I can't imagine what it would have been like if someone had come to her house and seen two people walking around with shower caps on their heads! But we did.

We watched the World Series. Back then, her television was a wood-covered box with an antenna sticking out the top. It looked like a blocky wooden insect. If the picture was fuzzy, we put aluminum foil on the antenna. We didn't have remote controls or voice activation; we had to get up from the couch and change the channel. And we didn't have flat-screen TVs you can hang on walls or watch in the palm of your hand. We had a wooden insect box.

The last month of her life, my grandmother's body was failing, and her bones and feet hurt. She couldn't walk, so she just lay on her couch in pain. But whenever she saw me, she smiled. Even with her pain, she was full of kindness. I remember seeing her frail body, knowing she was going away soon. She was close to leaving. It was like she had a living star inside her chest, shining through her pale blue eyes. And now that star was dimming.

I'm sure memories came for her too. I wonder what she thought about, lying there knowing she was close to the end. Maybe she thought of her parents, William and Emma. Maybe she thought of her husband, George, who passed nearly thirty years earlier. Maybe she thought of Nana and your great-aunt Dorothy and memories of being their mom. Maybe she thought of your uncle Bill and me too.

We are all memory carriers. Full of thoughts, emotions, and experiences given to us by those who loved us and cared for us. Memories of those we have loved. Memories from early childhood. Memories where we have been touched or moved in some way. Each of us carries personal memories and moments.

Hopefully we have memories to cherish like hidden treasures, reminding us we are loved, memories of experiences and places and friends and parents. I draw strength from my memories of my grandmother. I can still feel her love for me.

I remember where I was when she passed.

I was finishing graduate school in Chicago, driving home on the weekends to see her. Nana called me and told me she was going downhill. So I drove home, and then Nana and I drove to the hospital together. She passed minutes before we got there.

What do you do after someone you love passes away? What do

you say? No one prepares you for that. I wish I had been by her side, holding her hand, when she went. I saw her many times in the weeks leading up to the end.

When Nana and I got to the hospital, the doctor asked if we wanted to see her body. No. No, I didn't want to see it. I thought seeing her body would overwhelm me with grief. But something in me decided to go into her room while Nana stayed in the hallway. When I walked into her room, something felt different. It was unlike anything I've experienced before or since. I expected to lose control and cry, seeing the woman who helped raise me lying there. But when I walked into her room, she wasn't there. Even though her body was on the hospital bed, she wasn't there anymore.

Seeing her body gave me the real sense that she was gone. Surprisingly, it didn't feel sad. It felt hopeful. Powerful. She no longer needed me to carry her, bring her meals, take her to the beauty salon, or do anything for her. She was no longer in pain, no longer hurting or sad.

She was simply gone.

Walt Whitman once said there is nothing more beautiful than death. I'm not sure he was right, but there is beauty in the departure, beauty in her memory, beauty in the love she gave us, beauty in knowing she is home.

I walked into my grandmother's room expecting to fall apart, but I walked out filled with hope.

The next few days were a blur. *Tell friends. Write the obituary. Prepare for the funeral.* I picked out a casket for her. Light blue was her color. *Hold it together.* I wanted the funeral to be something she loved. I wanted to make her smile and honor her. I didn't know if she was watching, but I could feel her everywhere.

My grandmother's funeral was at her little church. Her husband, your great-grandfather George, donated the land for that church.

They wanted to hang a plaque on the wall with her name on it and asked me what Bible verses to put on it. There is a plaque hanging there for your great-grandfather too.

Her best friend, Lucille, played hymns on the organ. When it was time for me to share, I had a huge stack of the letters my grandmother had given me, and I read some of them. Everyone knew what a great woman she was, but I told them again anyway.

I told them how my grandmother loved me and my brother, how she raised us with her love and held up the sky for us. After her letters, I shared one of the verses I chose for her plaque. It's from John, where Jesus said, "I am the resurrection and the life. Whoever believes in me, though he die, yet shall he live, and everyone who lives and believes in me shall never die."

We were not created to die. It was not this way in the beginning. This is why death feels so wrong and confusing. Death was not part of the original plan; it was not in the blueprint. We were created for life. Death is here now, but it won't be forever. One day, there will be no more funerals or tears or goodbyes. This is all temporary.

My friend Charlie just came and sang some of his songs with us at the cabin. He wrote this one called "Death of Death," one of my favorites, in which he sings, "At the death of death You died and rose again."

We gathered around the life and legacy of my grandmother and were reminded that death does not have the final word. Death is not the end. My grandmother was no longer there. No longer in that hospital room, or in that casket a few feet from where I was speaking. She is alive, and she is home.

One day we will all be together,
Dad

CHAPTER 6
SONG

April 16, 2020

Dear Rosie, Dass, and Evangeline,

Tonight, we drove around looking for deer, listening to swamp frog songs, and singing in my truck: "You Make Me Brave," "Good Good Father," and "How He Loves." We rolled down the windows, turned up the music, and sang. I love listening to you sing.

Dass, my favorite picture of you is the one with you singing, arms stretched to the sky, reaching. It reminds me of trees. God could have designed them round or square or flat. But he made them tall, reaching strong and tender branches to the sky. They are rooted, and they are reaching. We, too, are created to reach.

We sometimes listen to the radio together. Millions of people sing these radio songs. It feels as if the whole world turns on these never-ending streambursts. Four-minute symphonies of desire, loss, joy, pain, love. Floating soul-pieces of longing. These pieces put words and language on unseen places, places too deep for reason or thought.

There is a story about a good man named Job who lost everything. He lost his possessions, his family, and even his health. After losing everything, he spoke with God, trying to make sense of it. God finally answered Job, saying, "Where were you when I laid the foundations of the earth . . . as the morning stars sang together and all the angels shouted for joy?"

Creation was born in song.

In the beginning, when light rushed into the void, when God spoke the earth, moon, and stars into existence, there was singing. There was shouting and roaring in the heavenly places, and joy filled every corner of the universe. And I believe pieces of this music, this creation Song, still exist today. Echoes from the one Albert Einstein called the "invisible piper."

Maybe the birds hear it every winter when they fly south.

Maybe the salmon hear it in the summer when they return to the streams.

Maybe the wolves hear it in the moonlight. Maybe our ears are just out of tune.

Echoes of the creation Song are all around us. And right now, there is a song being sung in heaven, a song we join when we lift our hearts and voices and reach. A song that was here in the beginning and will be forever.

King Solomon said God has put eternity in the heart of every person, and we feel this in our songs. Even when these longings are unmet. Tragedy tills the soil of our hearts for hope. Loss plants the seed of rediscovery. Heartbreak invites us to love again.

All our longings and all our songs point us to the one true Song.

Evangeline, you love playing a game we call "Spider." My hand becomes a skittering, running spider. He stands on the car seat or the ceiling of my truck, minding his own business. Sometimes when he is invited, he will climb onto someone's foot. But today, he was feeling extra. He probably ate too much sugar. He was dancing on the car seat, then jumped on my head, uninvited!

You were quietly watching all this, but when Spider jumped on my head, you erupted in laughter. I guess that just encouraged Spider, because he kept doing it over and over. When I looked up to see what you were laughing at, I couldn't see Spider. You were roaring and laughing and shouting, "Spider is on your head! He's on your head!" I never saw him, though. You laughed and laughed. When you laugh, the atmosphere changes. Everything feels lighter.

Maybe the Song also lives in the laughter of children.

Maybe the Song still lives in us, too, in our hearts and minds, in our blood and bone memory and every cell in our bodies. A UCLA scientist, Jim Gimzewski, made this discovery in 2001. Each of our bodies contains trillions of cells, and when Jim listened with his science instruments, he heard a song. He found that every cell in our bodies is saturated in Song. Maybe one day, someone will match these cell frequencies and use music to heal and repair our bodies.

Doctors have discovered that music lives in deep places in us. Music even lives in brains that have lost their memory. They have found that many people with dementia, who can no longer remember their names, can still sing songs and dance to the music. Music that they have not sung or even heard in decades. Music lives deep within us.

Scientists have been watching and listening to stars for decades.

They tell us that magnetars are a special kind of neutron star that send out sounds, pulses, radio frequencies, and radiation. These bursts are brief and powerful, and they can interrupt our radios here on earth. They call them "fast radio bursts" or FRBs. What if these outbursts are tiny, millisecond fragments of the creation Song? What would it sound like if billions of stars sang at the exact same time? Like "when all the morning stars sang together"?

I remember when I was eighteen, singing Christmas songs in a little chapel in Arkansas. For the first time, my heart began to reach, like Dass was reaching in that picture. I was a freshman in college. My friend Jon, who lived two doors down, was leading the songs. He was playing his guitar and singing with his eyes closed, not to us but to Someone Else. And for the first time, I did the same thing.

It is said, "God lives in the praises of his people," and I believe that means God meets us when we sing to him. As I sang to him, something deeper happened. Deeper than when I sang my radio songs. It was an awakening. And peace. It required trust to keep my heart open. I wish I could describe it better.

I didn't even realize I was crying. But they were not sad tears. It felt like when you hug someone and close your eyes and squeeze and forget everything around you. Comfort. Like when you've carried something heavy for a long time and finally put it down. Release. Now I know it was the Spirit of God touching, healing, and filling me.

I felt alive with these first new songs.

God is the Spirit inside us.

I love the verse that says, "Be filled with the Spirit" and the next line, "speaking to one another with psalms, hymns, and songs from the Spirit." There is a mysterious and certain relationship between our singing to God and being filled with the Spirit of God. And this is one reason why we meet together on Sunday mornings, raise our hearts and our voices, and sing.

After that night, I started playing Jon's guitar. (I still have that guitar. It's the one with the hole in it.) Jon taught me three chords, and I sat in his room for hours, playing those first new songs. I usually snuck in there when he was still in class or not around, and I played and sang. Singing as if God was in that dorm room, listening. And he was. For the next four years, I sang with him every Thursday night. There was no speaking, just singing with Jon, Zac, Stacy, Weaver, Durrett, Scottie, Tommy, Burris, and Gibson. Those moments changed me. My life was becoming a song.

My friend Don says our lives are stories. I think our lives are songs too.

I think we find the meaning of our lives when we hear and join the Song. When we reach with our hands and hearts and voices, our lives align with the frequencies of creation. And I think this is one reason God always calls for our songs. He knows we become like whatever we set our minds and hearts on.

When people close off their hearts to beauty and love, they become cold and stoic. Over time, their chilled hearts appear on their faces like stones. Others hold on to hurts, carrying negativity and bitterness. Their speech and their countenance become sour.

But if you live rooted and reaching, if you "set your [hearts] on things above, where Christ is, seated at the right hand of God. Set your minds on things above, not on earthly things," you stay open to all the possibilities of the supernatural. You stay open to everything you were created to be, to destiny and brilliance and light.

And your lives will become beautiful songs.

One day, you may find yourselves alone on a starless night. Shipwrecked and lost at sea. Maybe the shipwreck is of your own making. Life hasn't turn out as planned, and now despair is trying to wrap its dark tendrils around you, like some giant kraken to bring you down, down, down below. Maybe you have lost your song.

If those nights come, know I would do anything to be there with you, saying, "It's okay. Do not be afraid. I love you." Sit and rest. Pray.

Breathe. Invite a friend. Invite God. Cry if you need and as long as you need. "Those who sow with tears will reap with songs of joy."

And when you are able, remember to sing. Sing into the darkness. Sing into the depths. Sing when it hurts, when your throats are raw and you can't remember the words. The way back to your hearts is through song.

For you were created in Song, and to Song you return.

May your lives be beautiful songs,
Dad

CHAPTER 7
THANKFUL

April 30, 2020

Dear Rosie, Dass, and Evangeline,

We were riding bikes, and Eva, I asked if you wanted to ride without training wheels for the first time. You said, "Yes!" So I lowered the seat on Rosie's *Frozen* bike, and for the next two hours, I ran beside you, holding on to your handlebars as you pedaled as fast as you could. You were fearless. "Hey, biggies! Hey, biggies! Look at me!" you shouted to your sisters.

I'm so thankful for these moments. They are gifts. Every moment. Every bike ride. Every belly laugh. Every hello. Every goodbye. Every first guitar chord. Every first fish. Every first bike ride without training wheels. Every smile, heartbeat, blink, bite, and breath. Every moment is filled with ten thousand opportunities to be thankful.

Gratitude is knowing all of life is a gift.

As I write this, our country is still shut down because of the COVID-19 virus. Schools are closed. Libraries are closed. We are social distancing from friends. Gymnastics was canceled. Soccer was canceled, and we were bummed. We had recruited a great team; I was looking forward to coaching you on the Wolves.

One of my favorite authors, Ann Voskamp, wrote about the power of gratitude displayed by her family in the midst of hardship:

> No disaster, no storm, no cancellation, no termination, no catastrophe would stop them from giving thanks. . . .
> No matter where they were, every thanksgiving always brought them home—
> giving thanks, always bringing you home
> to the heart of God.

A few years ago, I went to Calcutta, India. In the morning, I drove to rural villages in a big green truck. Each truck in our group had a dozen large drums of hot food. Every time we stopped, there were long lines of people waiting for food. They stood and held out dented metal plates while we scooped hot rice meal onto them. That plate of food fed their families for the day.

Everyone smiled. Everyone was thankful. Not just in a habitual "thank you" way because they were supposed to say it. They were thankful in a deep-heart way. You could see it in their eyes, feel it in their smiles and relieved exhales. After giving them food, we stood with them on the dirt roads, and they circled us and smiled for a long time.

For them, food is not an option or choice; it is survival. They don't get to choose between chicken tenders, pepperoni pizza, or tacos. They choose between eating and not eating, between life and death. Yet they were grateful for what they had.

I think gratitude has a lot to do with perspective. We can be grateful or complain about what we don't have and what we feel like we deserve. We can find the positive in almost any situation, or we can find the bad. It's easier to feel grateful when life is going well but another thing to actively be grateful when life is hard. Feeling and being are different things. Gratitude is a choice to be, even when we don't feel like it.

Some people brood and gripe and live in negativity. Please don't do this. Hold your tongue. Complaints are a waste of words, oxygen, and energy. They change your inner monologue, and over time, they change the way you see the world. Complaints are dissonance in the Song. Out of tune and off-key. Complaining spoils the wonder of the moment. Cleo Wade said, "Complaints have no magic."

Nana was good at being thankful. So was my grandmother Helen. Every time I brought Nana dinner, ran an errand, or basically did anything, Nana always said thank you, and you could tell she meant it. And she did this with everyone. Every time I took my grandmother to church, she thanked me for driving her, thanked me for helping her onto the sidewalk and walking her into the building. For them, gratitude was a reflex.

Gratitude requires slowing down.

Gratitude and wonder are siblings. If wonder is opening ourselves to the magic around us, then gratitude is both an opening and a practice. Gratitude is an action; it is something we do. Gratitude is our intentional recognition of blessings. No matter what we feel, gratitude is choosing to see the good.

Gratitude, like wonder, can be spoiled with haste. With noise, hurry, crowds. These things often dominate us and our senses; they can stir us up, grab our attention, and stress us out. But gratitude changes our inner narratives.

Gratitude requires an awareness to what is here and now. It is easy to live in the regret of yesterday, feeling guilty or stewing in the bitterness of bad things that happened to us. And it is easy to live in the worry or anxiety of tomorrow. I've done that some. But nearly all those things I feared, things I spent hours worrying about, never happened. I wish I had those hours back.

My friend Rosanna—you call her the Other Rosie—told me she begins every morning by writing down in her planner three things she is grateful for. She starts the day with gratitude. She gave me the idea to start a gratitude journal. I hope you start one too.

Over time, gratitude becomes a rhythm.

Scientists have done studies showing how gratitude rewires our brains. Gratitude releases serotonin and dopamine, and our brains seek more and it becomes a habit. It creates pathways in our brains, lowers our stress, boosts metabolism, and helps us sleep better. One study in particular focused on writing out gratitudes, as with gratitude journals. The researchers divided people into three groups. The first group of people wrote down things they were grateful for, the second group wrote down negative things, and the third did not do any writing activity at all. Those who wrote out their gratitudes reported "significantly better mental health," which led to things like increased energy, attention, enthusiasm, and determination.

It's good to remember and be grateful.

I have so much to be thankful for.

I had an amazing mom, Nana, who worked three jobs for us and loved us well. Like you said, Dass, you never saw her buy or do anything for herself. She was always thinking of us. Always on the lookout for you, to make sure you had clothes and clean and combed hair. Rosie, she liked combing your hair. She was the Giving Tree.

I had an amazing grandmother, Helen, who raised us with kindness. Dass, you got your blue eyes from her and from Papaw. She took care of us when Nana had to work. I cannot remember a single moment of meanness from her. She was good and gentle.

I have you amazing girls. I love being your dad. I never knew how much I could love anyone until you. You are so bright and fun, smart and talented. You are growing into beautiful young ladies. I'm so proud of you, so glad you are in the world, and so grateful to be your dad.

I am grateful that God loves me. I am alive. I have breath, health, food, and a roof over my head. I have good friends. I have the opportunity to write books. I am thankful for all of it, even the hard times.

No matter what happens in your lives, I pray you stay grateful. Gratitude builds a beautiful home.

I'm so thankful for you,
Dad

PART 3

GROWING
YOUNG

CHAPTER 8
WONDER

May 1, 2020

Dear Rosie, Dass, and Evangeline,

A few years ago, I took you girls to an aquarium in California. You were smiling and laughing, and you ran inside as if you were being chased by unseen creatures of joy. You saw dolphins and red starfish and playful otters. Every time you made a discovery, you wanted me to see it, so you said, "Look at this, Dad! Look at this, Dad!"

Everything was alive and new.

But my experience at the aquarium was different. I was not beaming like you. Here I was, surrounded by swirling stars of fish, red, orange, yellow, and blue. But somehow, I missed them. I think I was in a hurry and ready to move on to the next thing.

As we get older, we can lose our sense of wonder. Life becomes familiar. *Oh yeah, I've seen that before.* Some children are in such a rush to grow up, they forget or lose things along the way. Wonder is often the first casualty.

I love how you girls see the world. As you grow, some people may try to shame you with phrases like "You're immature," or "Grow up." Reject them. I hope you never grow up or old. Grow young. Stay full of wonder.

Wonder is a way of seeing. Wonder is seeing with new vision and an open heart. Wonder is seeing for the first time and in slow fullness. It is the opposite of boredom and overfamiliarity. There is a freshness to it. Appreciation. Wonder unveils glory, reveals love, and moves your heart to share with others. Albert Einstein wrote,

> The most beautiful thing we can experience is the mysterious. It is the source of all true art and science. He to whom emotion is a stranger, who can no longer pause to wonder and stand rapt in awe, is as good as dead: his eyes are closed.

Wonder is an experience and a pursuit. Seeing and seeking beauty in unexpected and expected places, in every day and in everything. Wonder is why people stargaze, watch sunsets, listen to ocean waves. To see and feel and remember. English playwright Eden Phillpotts said, "The universe is full of magical things patiently waiting for our wits to grow sharper." William Blake added:

> To see a World in a Grain of Sand,
> And a Heaven in a Wild Flower
> Hold Infinity in the palm of your hand,
> And Eternity in an hour.

Wonder sees the world, heaven, infinity, and eternity all around us.

I think children are born full of wonder and imagination. Today, Eva, you did not put down your toy sword, not even when you went to bed. All day long, you slashed the air, dancing around, jumping and fighting invisible foes. You finally said, "Good night, sword," and then transformed into a floppy fish, refusing to be still until I wrapped you up like a burrito. Then you became a dancing burrito. Your imagination is relentless.

We are born with radiance and the unstoppable capacity for imagination. Maybe this is part of the imago Dei. There is an infinite quality to it. It is wild and expansive. For many adults, the radiance is buried under bills, work schedules, and mortgages. Most adults don't play or fingerpaint or have summer vacations. No more birthday wishes. No more blowing out candles. Most adults put down their swords and dreams and never pick them up again.

Evangeline, when you are on my shoulders at the cabin, you always listen for deer and ask about every sound. Every jagged cricket leg, hawk shrill, river splash. If I talk, you quickly shush me and remind me to listen. You listen with anticipation. You are a wonder hunter. I think we were all once wonder hunters.

Distraction pulls us away from wonder. Many people are sucked into the LED lights of a small digital screen. These screens can become a life-consuming distraction. Millions of people are addicted to them. Nothing else captures their attention. Not other people in the room. Not even seismic moments of wonder happening all around us.

I saw a picture of a man sitting on a boat in the ocean. He was staring at his iPhone when, suddenly, a humpback whale surfaced right next to him. But he was glued to his phone and missed everything. Not even a fifty-foot-long whale weighing sixty thousand pounds could get his attention!

We are addicted to distraction.

We are fixated by these screens. Hypnotized. We are passive receptors of thousands of images and messages, scrolling our days and our lives away. Or we are on social media, hoping for likes on our posts and pictures, in a frantic scramble for low-level fame. But we have lost our wonder and imagination. It has been sucked into a tiny screen. The screens capture and press the pause button on our imaginations. When we finally put down the screens, we feel tired and bored without the constant stimulation.

When we are distracted by screens, we miss everything.

To live in wonder is to pause. To live in wonder is to pay attention.

I remember my Arkansas summers, going to the library with my grandmother. I grew up loving books, just like you girls. The library was my favorite place. I fell in love with stories and the smell of old books. We were in the presence of books, and it was quiet and sacred. If you were loud, the librarian stared at you. If you were too loud, the librarian shushed you. *Shh! Be quiet; the books are listening.*

There were endless stories with faraway places to visit, monsters to battle, and heroes to meet. I left the library with armloads of books and fell headfirst into these stories. And I have lived much of my life buried in books. I have walked in Middle-earth. I have seen Narnia.

These places ignite our imaginations and invite us to create new things. Imagination is all around us. Every word we speak was born in someone's imagination. Shakespeare created some two thousand English words! Imagine the air we breathe. It fills our lungs, capillaries, and blood with oxygen. But who got to name it *oxygen*? Who had the authority for such things? And why do we use the scientific name? It feels sterile, tame. I understand the classification and study behind scientific names. But no one calls a great white shark by its scientific name, *Carcharodon carcharias*. I don't even know how to pronounce it.

What if *oxygen* is not its true name? What if there was another word, a secret name, given before the dawn of time? The Hebrew word is *ruah*, which means "wind, breath, spirit." I think that feels more accurate than *oxygen*. What if the divine breath blown onto dust to create life is the same air we breathe today? Held in place by gravity and sky and atmosphere on this spinning earth?

Imagine the cars on the road, the boats on the water, the jets in the air. Some are electric, but nearly all of them are driven by fossil fuels, ancient and decaying life buried deep underground. Fossil fuels are discovered, drilled, pulled out of the earth, and then put into fuel tanks. Even after thousands of years, these ancient plants and animals are still brimming with life, capable of ignition and explosion. Life is combustible.

Every dream and invention was born in someone's mind. Spaceships, solar power, horse saddles, telephones, and televisions were all invented by someone. Even my cabin and your treehouse. Before all these things were created, they were imagined. So dream big dreams. Imagine. Create. Inspire.

You girls were born in divine imagination, before the beginning of time. Every cell of your bodies bursting with life and energy. Your hair curly, wavy, and straight. Your eyes brown, blue, and green. Your minds made to see beauty and endless possibilities. Your hearts made for eternal relationship. And your imaginations give you the power to create, dream, make, and write, joining the same creative profession as the One who created you.

Stay young and full of wonder,
Dad

CHAPTER 9
BRAVE

May 5, 2020

Dear Rosie, Dass, and Evangeline,

Nana attended Little Rock Central High School in 1957, the same year President Eisenhower ordered one thousand troops to defend the Little Rock Nine.

These nine courageous students were the first Black students to attend the all-white Central High School. They were the first brave ones to end segregation in Arkansas. But there were angry mobs rioting around the school, racists who didn't think the Black students should attend. Somehow, they believed Black students were inferior to white students, just because of the color of their skin. When the Arkansas governor refused to act, it showed his compliance with the racists. So the president acted.

That year, Nana was a fifteen-year-old senior and editor of the school paper. She told me about how the armed soldiers followed the Black students around the school. Nana said you could always tell when one of the Nine was in the bathroom, because a soldier with a rifle was standing outside it, protecting them.

Nana knew that racism was wrong, and she had the courage to speak against it. That year, she and her coeditor wrote in the school paper, "We cannot be proud of the violence that occurred around our school that made it necessary for the use of these Federal troops. Looking back on this year will be with regret that integration could not have been accomplished peacefully, without incident, without publicity."

Nana spoke out, writing articles, standing up to local mobs and racists. For the rest of the year, the *New York Times* and other news outlets noted her bravery, publishing her words. Even at fifteen, she was fierce and brave.

There will be hard moments in your lives, moments that require courage. Moments that require you to be fierce and brave. You will need to stand. And sometimes you will need to stand up for others. I hope you rise. I hope you choose bravery even when standing up and speaking out costs you something.

A couple of years before the Little Rock Nine, another woman chose bravery. Her name was Rosa. She lived in Alabama, where the state had segregation laws, splitting up people because of the color of their skin. Separate water fountains. Separate bus seats. The whole thing was ignorant and sad. One day, Rosa was riding the bus. She paid and quietly sat in the "coloreds only" section, which was reserved for Black people.

When the bus stopped in front of the Empire Theater, more people boarded, and the bus driver decided to move the "coloreds only" section farther back. He asked Rosa to move. She refused and was arrested. She was arrested because she did not believe in an evil law that said Black people were lesser humans. When Rosa was asked about it, she said, "When that white driver . . . waved his hand and ordered us up out of our seats, I felt a determination cover my body like a quilt on a winter night."

Rosa became a face of the civil rights movement.

Sometimes courage is loud and public. Sometimes it is quiet resolve. Mary Anne Radmacher wrote, "Courage doesn't always roar. Sometimes courage is the quiet voice at the end of the day saying, 'I will try again tomorrow.'"

No great thing has ever been accomplished without courage.

A few years ago, I spent some time with Sister Rosemary Nyirumbe. Sister Rosemary has given her life for young women who have been scarred by war. She lives in Uganda and takes care of these girls, many of whom are orphans or have been abused or enslaved. *Time* magazine named her on their 100 Most Influential People list.

That night my friend Reggie and I were introducing her to speak. Reggie said a few things, and I spoke about her courage. How terrorists with machine guns came to her orphanage to steal the children, but Sister Rosemary stood her ground and refused. Even though she was unarmed and unable to defend herself, she was not afraid. The terrorists left her alone. She loves her children, and love fuels her courage.

Love fuels our courage. Remember, you are never too young to stand up and be brave. You are never too young for great acts of courage. People will look down on you or say you cannot do this or that or say you are just a girl, but you are never too young.

Sophie Scholl was a student at the University of Munich whose brave actions helped end World War II. And she was only a few years older than you are now.

Sophie graduated from high school and wanted to teach kindergarten. She was required to go through a Nazi brainwashing training course. She was also studying the Christian theologian Augustine at the time. The more she read and understood, the more she realized the Nazi invasions and war crimes were horribly wrong. So she stood up and spoke out.

Sophie joined a resistance group called the White Rose, a nonviolent movement to stop the Nazis. The group members wrote six small books and distributed thousands of copies, sounding the alarm, calling the Nazis' war evil and calling people to action.

After she was captured and sentenced to death, Sophie did not waiver, saying, "I did the best that I could do for my nation. I therefore do not regret my conduct and will bear the consequences."

To this day, Sophie and the White Rose are revered in Germany.

Whatever you set out to do in your lives, it will require courage. Even dreaming requires courage. It will be hard. It may be costly. You may feel afraid. Courage is not the absence of fear; it is doing the right thing even when you feel afraid. Courage doesn't mean you always win; it means you get up and try again, even when you fail. And remember: You are not alone. God is with you. You girls are growing into women of courage.

I believe in you,
Dad

CHAPTER 10

BEAUTIFUL

May 10, 2020

Dear Rosie, Dass, and Evangeline,

You girls know Ms. Dianne. She is kind. And not just in the surface way. Not like those who dress up and smile at parties but are mean at home. Ms. Dianne is kind in her bones. She is kind to everyone she meets. Gentle and strong. She raised four children, adopted another, and has spent years helping people in need. When you're around her, you can feel her peace. When she smiles, you feel warmth radiating from her.

When I think of beautiful people, Ms. Dianne comes to mind. She has spent her life making good choices, choosing kindness, light, and love. She quietly chooses beauty, and by choosing beauty, she becomes it. After years of choosing beauty, it resides in her eyes and heart, resting on her head like an invisible crown.

Beautiful is something you are and something you become.

Beauty is hard to put into words. Sometimes it is seen dancing between lines of poetry or songs. But mostly, like the sun, it is too brilliant to behold. You have to look sideways at it, peeking through your fingers. Beauty makes you shield your eyes.

Beauty is something you see and feel. It is something you remember. Somewhere deep in our cells, hidden in some lost language, is a longing for beauty. This longing is an eternal one, bursting with divine things, with Paradise Lost and Will-Be-Found, with the farewell and the return. Beauty calls us home.

Beauty is alive, shimmering with movement. It is not passive, not just something to look at, like a gold-framed painting in a museum. It is active. Moving and breathing. It creates and replicates, blooming on the surface and in the hearts of everyone it touches.

Beauty is advocacy. Calling us to something infinite, to Someone radiant and full of glory. Beauty does not wilt or surrender in the never-sleeping darkness. Beauty is stern and unyielding. Like the White Tree of Gondor, blooming defiantly in the face of shadow.

Beauty hovers over all of us, existing in our darkness and our light. It exists in the withered frailty of life. In the breathless triumph of death. Beauty lies in our sleeping and waking, our innocence and tragedy. Beauty is found in small, unseen gestures of love, humming softly in every act of kindness. Beauty is everywhere.

You are beautiful. You are made in the image of the beautiful God. Words can be ugly. Choices can be ugly. Actions can be ugly. Some people make ugly choices and develop ugly character. But all people, in their created essence, are beautiful.

The world will try to define beauty for you. They will say beauty is a product to purchase. *Buy this; become beautiful.* They spend billions of dollars trying to convince you, telling you to add something to your lives to become beautiful. They say beauty is found in an object, like a dress or makeup. They say beauty is an image to become. They will bombard you with images on your phone, on your computer, on televisions, and in magazines. Saying you need to buy or change something to be beautiful.

Here's a secret: You don't need to buy or change anything. Beauty is a heart to cultivate and a character to develop. Like Ms. Dianne.

There are many pretty faces, models on the covers of magazines and stars in movies. There is nothing wrong with being pretty or wanting to be pretty, and I like buying you dresses and fingernail polish. But beauty is deeper, stronger, and more enduring than pretty. And some people with pretty faces have ugly hearts.

At the pinnacle of creation, God made man and woman in his image. He created you as a holy reflection, a walking, breathing, laughing, divine reflection. And I believe he made you to say something specific, to echo something about who he is inside your heart and outside to the world. I believe it is this holy word on repeat, whispering, "Beautiful, beautiful, beautiful."

We are beauty reflectors, changed from glory to glory. His beauty shines on us when we lift our hearts and hands. Our brief and fragile lives are splintered reflections of infinite and immortal beauty.

Some of the most beautiful creatures go through the harshest struggles. They often come out of the struggle changed. Born again. Beautiful. Someone once said that we marvel at a butterfly's beauty but seldom ponder the changes it has gone through to become beautiful. Without a cocoon, there would be no butterfly.

Flowers, too, are buried before they can bloom. Diamonds are formed under intense pressure and heat. Gold is purified by fire. No struggle, no diamond. No fire, no gold. In the same way, your beautiful life is formed through heat, pressure, and struggle. Struggle will come in different forms. Unfulfilled dreams. Lost relationships. Betrayal. Pain. I don't wish this for you. But I've lived long enough to know the truth of Jesus: "In this world you will have trouble." Struggle is your opportunity for growth and beauty.

But struggles can have a negative effect; some people never get over them. Some people choose to be bitter. They nourish those negative thoughts. They blame and lash out at others. Some people stay bitter. They live in the struggle, even if it happened years and decades ago. For the rest of their lives, they carry the struggle as their story, the story they tell themselves and others. But others forgive, learn wisdom, and emerge from the struggle humbler and more beautiful. As Elisabeth Kübler-Ross wrote,

> The most beautiful people we have known are those who have known defeat, known suffering, known struggle, known loss, and have found their way out of the depths. These persons have an appreciation, a sensitivity, and an understanding of life that fills them with compassion, gentleness, and a deep loving concern. Beautiful people do not just happen.

We are made and marked by struggle. Sometimes we are even scarred by it. The scars are quiet reminders of the pain and the process, poor choices and failures. My struggles have left me more accepting and less judgmental of others and myself, more grateful for my friends and the grace of God. One of my favorite writers, my friend Myquillyn Smith, wisely said, "It doesn't have to be perfect to be beautiful."

Beautiful is something you are and something you become.

You are beautiful,
Dad

PART 4

BECOMING

CHAPTER 11

SEEDS

June 11, 2020

Dear Rosie, Dass, and Evangeline,

Sometimes when I need a place to think, I walk among these old pecan trees and think of my great-grandfather who planted them, my grandfather who tended them, and my grandmother who lived here with him in a redbrick house. I used to visit as a boy. Nana wrote poetry here, spoke Latin, and climbed these trees. Aunt Dorothy climbed these trees too. I walk here and remember the goodness they gave to me. Their memories root me and give me strength.

Every evening, the sun lowers gently into the west. Dusky light shines through these branches, and the ground comes alive, crawling with leafy shadows. Sometimes the light is soft and muted. Sometimes it looks like everything is ablaze with orange fire. Then the sky darkens midnight blue, purple, and black.

In the fall, pecans lie on the grass. In the winter, the trees are barren and empty. But soon, spring comes and the green blooms in the trees, and the birds return to sing again. The cold haze of winter melts into spring. And some people have a spring too.

Years ago, these trees were little brown-shelled pecans. Planted in the earth, watered and sprouted green and tender in the sunlight. They took root and grew tall and deep. You plant things too. You plant seeds in your lives. Thomas Merton said, "Every moment and every event of every man's life on earth plants something in his soul."

The ideas you think.

The affections you feel.

The thoughts you nourish.

The imaginations you dream.

All these things are seeds. The seeds you water grow to become the words you speak, the decisions you make, the patterns you form, which ultimately become your character, which is who you are, who you really are. Your lives have the same rhythm as these pecan trees. Seed. Plant. Water. Grow. Bloom. Harvest.

Most young people spend their lives rushing from home to school to back home, activity to activity. They don't imagine how the seeds planted now will take root, grow, and bloom in their lives. They wake and sleep and live every day with no deep reflection on who they are becoming.

It's good to prepare for college and the workforce, to memorize and to learn the discipline that study requires. It is good to learn how to work hard for a goal and pass a test. It is good to learn how to interact with your teachers and peers and friends, how to be a team player, how to listen and absorb information. These lessons, perhaps more than the information itself, will stay with you all your lives and serve you well.

Most people graduate and enter the professional world; take on internships, jobs, and careers; build résumés and skills and work experience and references. When meeting a new person, most adults ask this question first: "What do you do?" They ask about your job, your external life. Many people never ask or think about the deep questions, like "Who are you?" Many people never ask that question of themselves.

Who am I? Who am I becoming?

The last few letters have been about internal things. Gratitude. Wonder. Courage. These things shape your character, how you live and interact with the world and others and God.

The first thing that shapes us is the decisions we make in every moment.

You forge your character through millions of small decisions. One bad decision does not break you or define you. *Character*, according to Gordon MacDonald, "is a word that describes the default 'me.' The person I am over the long haul in life. The person who emerges in the most difficult, challenging moments. Character identifies the attitudes, convictions, and resulting behaviors that distinguish my life. . . . Character is what people can expect of me in *most* situations."

This is a grace-filled view of character. Your reputation can be damaged in a moment, but the moment does not make or break you. Even if you feel like you failed horribly, you are not a failure.

Character is who you are over the long haul.

Our character starts as children. *Do I share my favorite toy or dress, or do I hoard it for myself? Do I make kind or rude and mean choices? Do I tell the truth to my parents? Do I forgive my sister? Do I apologize and change? Do I have a thankful heart? What seeds am I planting in my life?*

Wisdom is making good and godly choices with your lives. Someone can be highly intelligent but not wise. In the Bible, James wrote, "The wisdom that comes from heaven is first of all pure; then peace-loving, considerate, submissive, full of mercy and good fruit, impartial and sincere."

Wisdom is peaceful. Wisdom is slow. Wisdom considers. Wisdom listens.

I've seen people plant, water, and reap the seeds of their decisions. One girl I knew for twenty years was full of compassion and had a rare sensitivity about her. But as a teenager, she started sowing bad seeds, being harsh and using people. And slowly, over time, she changed. She became callous and uncaring about who she hurt. She created a victim narrative about herself that made everyone else the bad guy, and when anyone disagreed, she cut them off. She didn't look anything like that kind girl anymore.

Every decision we make changes us.

Another major player in your becoming is the story you tell yourselves.

Your thoughts are seeds. Many people live unaware of their own internal monologues and thought lives. People create and make situations inside their minds. Sometimes they are based on truth; sometimes they are not. Someone once said, "Your words create your world," and this is especially true of the words we tell ourselves, the stories we nourish in our minds. Over time, our beliefs can become our reality.

People interpret situations and have real feelings attached to their interpretation. The feelings are true and accurate, even if the interpretation is not accurate. Do not jump to conclusions or make premature assumptions about others. Be careful about opening a whole can of feelings over a situation before you know if your interpretation is true.

When bad things happen, don't be afraid of big feelings or tears. It's okay. But don't ruminate on negative thoughts. Don't stew on the bad things people have done to you and get bitter. Don't keep rehearsing personal failures over and over again. Don't give shame power over you. Learn from it, pray, let go, and move on. Release and be free.

If you live complaining and speaking of your losses, ruminating on bitterness, hurts, and negativity, you will become these things. But if you live grateful and speak life, if you meditate in your hearts on "whatever is true, whatever is noble, whatever is right, whatever is pure, whatever is lovely, whatever is admirable—if anything is excellent or praiseworthy," you become these things. Be mindful of the stories you tell yourselves and the stories you tell others about yourselves.

You can control the story you tell yourselves. Turn off the negative voices. Don't reinforce them with complaining. Diffuse them with gratitude. Be grateful. God loves you. You have two parents who love you, grandparents, aunts, uncles, cousins, and friends. Keep doing your best at school and home and life. I'm proud of you.

Many young people limit themselves by negativity or fear, saying, "I could never do that." Others create a conformist narrative and are just trying to fit in, trying to be cool or popular. A lot of teenagers do this. They are consumed by worry about what everyone else thinks.

When we live in fear of others, we never become who we were born to be.

Your lives are open, untouched soil. The seeds you sow now, and later as teenagers and young adults, will bloom in your lives. Plant good seeds. It is much easier to plant good seeds than to uproot weeds after they are grown. Over time, these seeds become your character, which is who you are, who you really are.

> Your lives are becoming a
> beautiful landscape,
> Dad

CHAPTER 12

FINGERPRINTS

June 22, 2020

Dear Rosie, Dass, and Evangeline,

When we first brought Shadow to the cabin, he was an indoor cat. He had never explored the outdoors, climbed a tree, chased a squirrel or a rabbit.

For the first few weeks, he stayed in the basement. Evangeline, you would call him, "Shaaa-dow, Shaaa-dow." He tiptoed out to be petted, then ran back to the basement and hid under the couch, peering out with yellow eyes. Every day, he went a little farther. Under the treehouse, then around the cabin, then chasing a cricket into the woods. The first night he spent outside, I left the basement door open, just in case. The next morning I went outside, he walked up purring. He could have slept inside but chose to stay out in the wild.

Then I started finding dead mice around the cabin. This could not be our timid, sweet Shadow; he was no killer. But last night, Dass, you caught a mouse, and when you put it down, Shadow pounced, carried off the mouse, and ate him! Then Shadow stalked a deer and tried to pounce on him. Our sweet, feather-chasing kitten was now a dark hunter. How did this happen? How did he transform from a sweet kitten into a hunting cat?

How do we transform?

Some of our transformation comes from the choices we make. Some we inherit, in our minds and bodies and brains. Scientists refer to this as "nature" in the nature-versus-nurture debate. Some is instinct. Like Shadow's change into a hunting cat without any of our help. Some is environment. Some is supernatural. Each of us is created with unseen imprints. Soul fingerprints waiting to be discovered. Song lines written into us before the beginning of the world. Of the billions of people who crawl, walk, run, and stoop with two legs, none are alike.

One of the great joys in life is discovering your soul fingerprint, how God made you. We all have a unique blend of personality, decisions, talents, gifts, and traits. But many people never discover who they are made to be.

Secretly, many people are unhappy and discontent with their lives, relationships, and jobs. Something feels amiss, but they cannot put it into words. They are discontent because they are not functioning within their design. They never learned who they are and are now trying to be someone they are not.

As a child, I spent years creating, writing, and reading stories. I wrote my first book on planets when I was in third grade. Dass and Rosie, you wrote your first books in second grade! Many of my early days in class were spent drawing pictures and passing them to my friend J. D. (Do not draw pictures in class and pass them to your friends!)

J. D. and I drew each other in unfortunate situations. Once he drew a giant trying to eat me on a spoon! So I drew him being swallowed by a megalodon. The top of his pictures always said, "Poor

John." Mine said, "Poor J. D." Thankfully, none of these unfortunate events ever came true. Now, we are both happy, semi-functioning adults.

I continued to read and draw and write throughout high school and college. When my grandmother passed, I read *The Hobbit* and The Lord of the Rings. I connected with the vulnerable hobbits and the doubting Strider. There was grief and loss but also light and love. Walking in Middle-earth left on me a residue of hope, an elvish magic. This inspired me to start writing a fiction book. Maybe I'll finish it one day.

But for some reason, right after I graduated college, I abandoned art and writing and all those things I loved. I directed a homeless shelter, worked in prisons, helped with at-risk youth. I loved the relationships, but I'm not created for details and tasks. I don't even remember where I put my car keys. Like right now, I don't know where my keys are. My heart felt buried under it all.

One guide that helped me discover my personality is called the Enneagram. It describes nine different personality types, helping you understand yourself. It also helps you learn about other people, how they deal with shame and interact. It showed me a lot about myself as a Type Four, with its hopes and challenges. I found it to be surprisingly accurate. It gave me permission to be myself. And when I moved away from my fingerprint, it helped me come back to myself again.

You girls are smart and gifted, and people will recruit you. Causes will want you to join them. Companies will try to hire you. People, sometimes even friends and family, will try to squeeze you into doing and being what they think you should be. Some people may try to push their unrealized dreams onto you. No. There is freedom in finding who you were created to be.

Finding your soul fingerprints comes as you grow and make new discoveries. This is the greatest joy: being who you are. Don't worry about being popular, whether people approve or not. Do the thing you feel created to do. This gives you deep joy and freedom that have nothing to do with what people say.

For me, this is being a creative person and writing. I try to write words impressed on me. C. S. Lewis said, "I never exactly made a book. It's rather like taking dictation." I try to do this. I listen. I feel. I write. I try to find the soul of the thing; then the words come. I try to be faithful to the work. Then I celebrate and rest.

When you receive feedback from others, listen to people you respect and trust. They will affirm you and call things out in you. Your personalities, gifts, and talents are still developing. You are exploring, finding passions and things you love. Discover who you are. Fight for it. Fight to become it. Don't wait for permission from anyone; do what you feel called to do, be who you are called to be.

I love who you are becoming,
Dad

PS: I see some things in you girls and will share a few of them now. These are suggestions, so don't take them as universal truths. You are young and changing, so hold my words loosely. (Please turn to the back of the book to read your personal letters, then join me back here.)

CHAPTER 13

NORMALS

July 4, 2020

Dear Rosie, Dass, and Evangeline,

I grew up in a house without internet, without a computer or a cell phone, but with a lot of love and laughter. In the summers, I rode my bike down to the swimming pool. The family listened to music. Records. Johnny Cash. Kenny Rogers. Willie Nelson. We read books. Nana had a wall of books in her living room. Music and books were treasures. Words mattered. Songs mattered. Stories mattered.

We went to church on Sunday mornings. And about once a month, I went to All Souls with my grandmother. Nana loved to travel and take pictures of her trips. She tried to see things from a different angle and capture the perfect shot. She encouraged my art; framing and hanging up my drawings of hawks and ducks and other creatures. Art and beauty were celebrated and displayed.

These things became my normal, and I still carry them with me. I didn't understand it when I was a boy, but most of the things that Nana valued and celebrated are the same things I value and celebrate today. Her values shaped my normal. How people see and relate to the world is their normal.

You have a normal too.

If we lived in London, you girls might have British accents. Or if we still lived in New York, we would take the subway instead of owning and driving cars. Or if we lived a hundred years ago, we might live on a farm and make our living from the crops. But today, you attend good schools, have opportunities to play sports, go to good doctors and dentists, shop at clean grocery stores, and have a house and your own beds.

Your cousins live in Burundi and have far different normals than you. Tonight we shot fireworks at the cabin and celebrated the Fourth of July. Where your cousins live, they have a different history and don't shoot fireworks. In the United States, we take internet and air-conditioning and clean water for granted. They don't always have electricity or clean water.

You are learning and absorbing new things every day. Some you are aware of; some you are not. You learn from your environment, from your parents and family and friends and culture. The friends you choose influence your normals and who you become. John Donne wrote, "No man is an island, entire of itself; every man is a piece of the continent, a part of the main."

Friends influence how you speak, interact, and react; your value system; how you view God, yourself, and others; how you think, feel, and make decisions. Your friends will change your lives. So choose wisely. Someone said, "Show me your friends, and I'll show you your future," and I think that's true.

Your lives and your destinies are connected to those around you. We take on our friends' habits, values, what they care about. We take on their outlooks and perceptions, how they treat and speak of others. If our friends are negative and critical, we may find ourselves being more negative and critical of others. If they are kind, we may be more kind. King Solomon wrote in Proverbs, "Walk with the wise and become wise, for a companion of fools suffers harm."

Every year I was in college, I watched teenagers make their first choices away from their parents. They were fresh out of high school, out of their homes, taking their first new steps as young adults. They made new friends, joined social clubs, went to classes. These choices affected who they were becoming.

Some teenagers wanted acceptance so much that they were willing to do anything to fit in. Some made decisions they would never have made a few weeks earlier at home. Some stayed out too late with friends, oversleeping and missing classes. Others wasted their money on gambling and substances, and they formed addictions. Some failed classes or quit altogether.

In most cases, the students were influenced by the new friends they chose. It was almost a certainty, if someone was doing poorly, acting foolish, and making bad choices, they were not making these choices alone. In almost every case, they made these choices under the influence, pressure, and guidance of their new friends. Many of these students came into college as freshmen with good intentions, but they wilted under pressure from new friends and made bad choices.

Your friends influence who you become. When you attend junior high, high school, and college, I hope you hold on to yourself and your character. I pray you do not wilt under pressure and you have the courage to do what is right, even if you are the only ones. I hope you remember who you are.

People interpret life through their environments and experiences, and, especially, through the pain they have felt. Many people live as reactions to their normal. Maybe they grew up hurt or controlled or just didn't like things about their childhood. They say, "When I grow up, I will never do that." They think they are making a break from their normal. But their whole lives are a reaction to it.

Maybe you're seeing me act a certain way now, and decades later, when you are married, you'll remember your childhood experience and believe, *This is how men are supposed to act.* You may feel disappointment if a man doesn't have a beard or cook you special pancakes or do things the way your dad did. Your childhood experiences often become the framework for what you expect in your adult lives and relationships. Some values are a foundation on which to build your lives. Other values can become prisons.

Your childhoods give you images and emotions that feel like home. For the rest of your lives, you may seek friendships, professions, and, one day, husbands based on these images and emotions. If something feels comfortable and feels like home, you may even accept it without further thought. Many people believe, *This is the way it was in my life; this is the way it should be.*

As you grow older, it is important to learn how to step outside of yourself and look at things as an objective observer. People call this self-awareness. With age you begin to see your normals from a different perspective and even create new ones. As you grow up, take the positives from your normals and embrace them. Discard the negatives and replace them with something of your own making. You will build your own normals. You have the grace and power to build them. You can design the blueprints. You are the architects.

> What you build can be anything,
> Dad

CHAPTER 14

WHISPERS

July 22, 2020

Dear Rosie, Dass, and Evangeline,

Every night around nine o'clock, you girls go to sleep, and every morning, you crawl out of bed, ready for a new day. Scientists say our bodies, brains, and cells heal when we sleep. When it gets dark, our bodies begin to shut down, and when we fall asleep, our brain patterns change. There is rest and regeneration.

Every human keeps this same pattern. But why did God make us to sleep? Why couldn't he have just left us awake all the time? I'm not sure; it's a mystery. But I do see contrasts. Work and rest. Darkness and light. Old and new. Maybe sleep is a reminder of our dependency and finiteness. There may be some connection to "his mercies are new every morning." To the daily creation rhythm of "there was evening, and there was morning." And to the weekly creation rhythm of "on the seventh day he rested."

The lifespan for the average American is seventy-nine years. Which means, on average, we wake up 28,854 times in our lives, including leap years. We wake from sleep thousands of times, but there are few times our souls awake. These supernatural moments can change our lives.

There is a spiritual aspect of your becoming. Your decisions shape you. Your fingerprints shape you. Your normals shape you. And the Spirit shapes you. The same Spirit who hovered over the waters at the creation of the world is hovering over your lives to awaken you, create you, fill you, and make you new.

I remember going to a Billy Graham meeting when I was in tenth grade. Coach Smith took our football team to hear him speak. There was singing. Then Billy spoke. Billy was warm and kind, and even though the stadium was full of people, it felt like he was speaking directly to me. I agreed with him in a deep-heart way. I knew he was right. There was no pleading or pressuring. He was saying God loved me and was inviting me into a relationship with him.

As a high schooler, I didn't think much about these things. I thought about friends and family, football and baseball. More than sports, I wanted the older guys on the team to like and accept me. I went to youth group, the youth pastor was a good man named Mark. He was always smiling and happy to see me; he always called me "bro." But I didn't think much about spiritual things. I believed in God and knew he loved me, but I didn't have a relationship with him.

But that night, Billy Graham's message pierced me. It seemed like God was whispering to me, and I heard him. I was sleepwalking through life and was now awake. The message was simple, and I believed it. I still believe it. And when Billy invited us into a relationship with God, it was an easy decision. Everything inside me said yes. I know you girls have said yes too.

After that night, Billy mailed me a book called *Peace with God: The Secret of Happiness*. I read it every night before I went to bed. God was making these things come alive in me. The next few years, I learned to depend on him and seek him.

There is a verse in Psalms that says, "God whispers to those who trust him." This means he shares his heart with us like a best friend. And we can share our hearts with him too. As I opened my heart to God, it began to change. Everything expanded. The world got bigger. I started caring about more than just my life, my sports, and my friends. I began thinking and caring deeply about others and the world.

There was a young boy named Samuel who was around the age you girls are now. One night, Samuel lay down to sleep in the place they called the house of God, when he suddenly heard a whisper.

Samuel

After some confusion, Samuel opened his heart and listened. God spoke to him, gave him a calling, and was with him. God also whispered to the prophet Elijah when was he was afraid and hiding in a cave. God told Elijah that he was not alone.

When God whispers to you, make sure to listen and respond. Listen with an open heart, like Samuel did. I don't know who I would be today if I did not listen and respond when Billy Graham was speaking, over twenty years ago. That night was a rare and supernatural moment; it changed the trajectory of my life.

Sometimes God whispers to us in the darkest places. Sometimes he leads us there, to the desert, where we can no longer see or feel. Sometimes we lose our sense of sight, like Saul of Tarsus did, and we can only hear.

I was in the dark for a couple of blurry years. I don't remember them. I think it's because I was crushed under the weight of some unspeakable grief, and my mind and body just shut down as a response.

I remember lying in bed under thin sheets that sometimes didn't cover my feet. I remember calling friends and falling apart with tears and rambling nonsense. I remember sitting in the back of the coffee shop, wearing sunglasses so people couldn't see my bloodshot eyes. I remember Gail saying I was curled up in the fetal position. That's what I felt like: bent over and crumbling under the weight of it all.

Grief came in waves, like when the ocean is too strong, and it keeps knocking you over or pulling you farther out. Like it did to me that time when the ocean pulled me far out from the shore. I screamed and waved my arms for help, but no one saw. Then I finally found a giant coral reef and stood up on it and tried to walk. But I tripped and fell and cut myself. I made it out, but not without much falling, blood, and jagged scars.

The worst part of that season was feeling abandoned by God. Maybe I deserved it. But it didn't feel that way. It felt like it was his fault. I didn't sign up for this. When you go forward and commit your life to Christ, you are supposed to have a good life. You are not supposed to lose things, to lose loved ones, to lose promises and all the things you wanted in the span of a year or two. To lose even yourself. And for some reason, I thought it was all God's fault.

If you find yourselves in those places, be still and listen. Cry if you need and as long as you need. Get brutally honest. Get a couple of close friends. Get alone. Whispers come in stadiums or large, crowded places. But sometimes they come when we are quiet and alone or hiding in the back of a coffee shop or lying in bed, crushed by grief.

He is there. And he is inviting us to get honest, even if all we can do is show up. He whispers and reminds us that we are not alone. Sometimes he says, "It's okay, it's okay." Sometimes he says to come home. So open your ears. Open your hearts. Whispers are not usually audible, but they feel like peace.

> Keep your ears and your
> hearts open,
> Dad

CHAPTER 15
FILLED

July 24, 2020

Dear Rosie, Dass, and Evangeline,

I wish I could tell you how good it feels when you girls first see me. When I pick you up from school and you smile and shout, "Dad!" Then you laugh and run and crash into me and squeeze my legs and say, "I love you, Daddy." I say, "I love you too." These are my favorite moments. Before you were born, I never knew I could love someone as much as I love you now.

I used to think home was a place. Now I know home is a people.

In the last chapter, we talked about God's whispers. How God invites us into the home of his heart, and we invite him into ours. Some people call this "being filled with the Spirit." I think being filled with the Spirit is like coming home.

Home is where we are accepted, celebrated, loved, and known. Home is where we always have a room. Home is where we are always welcome. Like when I see you girls. Joy and affection comes bursting out with hugs and happy tears. A thousand beautiful reunions.

As in any relationship, we need to stay connected. Not because it's something we "should" do. But staying connected to God is good, deeply good. He wants to fill your lives with good things, gifts and ideas and visions and dreams that you cannot imagine. If you stay connected and walk in the Spirit, this will happen.

You may be tempted to gloss over this letter or think it sounds too spiritual. If it's not something you have experienced yet, you might be tempted to skip or dismiss it. But trust me when I say this is real. It's real. The God who made your family and friends and everyone in history is real and wants to know you in the most pure and deep way. He wants to take residence in your hearts and fill your lives with good things. For "in him we live and move and have our being."

In my own life, there were seasons when I was connected and close to God. And there were seasons when I stumbled and went against his direction and heart. I regret the times I did not stay close.

I do remember one season in college, and just after, when it felt like I was filled by the Spirit. It felt like he was living in my heart and veins and was bursting out of every pore of my body.

I remember singing every week with Jon and lifting my hands and heart. I haven't lifted my hands like that in a long time. There's freedom in it.

I remember reading a book about the Holy Spirit by a preacher named Chuck Swindoll. In the book, Chuck wrote out a prayer and explained how he prays and asks God to fill him every day. Chuck said God answers that prayer in his life. So I tore out that page, taped it to my dorm wall, and prayed it every morning. I think God answered it. I need to find that book again.

My friend Stacy used to pray and sing with Jon and me. Every week she showed up early and prayed that God would awaken people and change their lives. I was one of those people. Part of who I am today is because Stacy has prayed for me. She prays for lots of people. She doesn't make a show of it. She's humble. I respect her wisdom; it has been learned and earned through years of prayer. I asked her to tell me what it means to be filled with the Spirit. She said,

Walking in the Spirit is a rhythm. A choice we make every day. I wish I could say I walk in the Spirit every day. But on most days, I choose other things. Busyness, selfishness, anger, lust, greed. These are often my default choices; then I complain to God about my misery! But I always see his grace pursuing me, even in the midst of my wandering.

Walking in the Spirit is a relational connection. I connect with God through nature and worship and music. Every morning I try to go outside and pause. To look and listen. I try to take deep breaths, which is often hard in the Arkansas humidity. Nature reminds me of God's beautiful creation and how he provides for us.

Walking in the Spirit requires us to know the truth. I have read the Bible for most of my life. But this is the first year I learned to use the truth to combat the lies in my head and heart. I used to listen to the lies of my insecurities and the lies of others. Saying I am not good enough as a friend, as a wife, or as a mother. But now I am speaking the truth out loud, as a confession. And it is changing me. I memorize the Scriptures. I've learned that memorizing Scripture gives the Holy Spirit a vocabulary to speak into my life.

During the day, I listen to worship music. Loud on days when I am happy or mad, quiet on days when I am anxious. I play it continually and through the night when I can't sleep. I know there are many ways to connect with God, whether by social action, daily habits, quiet reflection. We all connect with God in our own personal way.

Walking in the Spirit is something we do together in community. I've learned that I need to be surrounded by a few people who have seen me at my worst and still love me and give me grace. When I am alone, I am more vulnerable to lies and unhealthy patterns. We were not created to walk this journey alone but to walk together.

I agree with Stacy. When I am connected, good things are formed in my heart. Love. Joy. Peace. Patience. Kindness. Goodness. Faithfulness. Gentleness. Self-control.

I can be some of these things on my own. But I have limits. And the Spirit can do things in me that I cannot do myself. On one hand, we are eternal image bearers of God, created in his goodness, capable of immense beauty. We all carry remnants of Eden. But we are conflicted. This eternal image has been tainted. This is the tragedy of the human story. We are fallen.

My defaults are my fallen nature. I am capable of personal treason. I am a threat to betray me. Paul shared his inner conflict, saying, "I do not understand what I do. . . . I do not do the good I want to do, but the evil I do not want to do—this I keep on doing."

I see the same conflict in my life. When I do not live surrendered, the fruit of the Spirit is absent from my life. It is slowly replaced by the weeds of the flesh. Impatience. Selfishness. Discontent. Envy. Lust. Unrest. Laziness. Pride. These are my defaults.

But when I surrender, the weeds are pulled and new seeds are planted in my heart. Over time I begin to look and act more like Jesus. Over time the fruit of the Spirit is my default. My new life starts with daily surrender. I can hurry to look at my phone, check social media, read the news, jump into the busyness of the day, and miss the connection with God. On these days, my insides feel unsettled. On these days, I am less patient and less at peace.

I wish I knew about this earlier, when I was your age.

If I was going to give you one gift from this book, one letter for you girls to read and reread, it would be this one. I can tell you things. I can tell you to be kind; I can model it and demonstrate it for you. I can give you "kindness treats." But I do not have the power to change your hearts into kindness. Only God can do that.

I've found one of the best times to connect with him is in the morning. There is something magical about the morning. The world is still and calm and holding its breath. It is filled with anticipation. "Early in the morning, Jesus went to a solitary place to pray."

C. S. Lewis wrote, "It comes the very moment you wake up each morning. All your wishes and hopes for the day rush at you like wild animals. And the first job each morning consists simply in shoving them all back; in listening to that other voice, taking that other point of view, letting that other larger, stronger, quieter life come flowing in. And so on, all day."

Like Lewis said, every day, you have a choice. You can stumble into the day, or you can wake and pause. Connect and remember who you are. When you do this, you discover all the gifts and graces and fruits that come with the connection. You become more like God. Your lives have a whole different trajectory.

Stay connected,
Dad

PART 5

DEVELOPING
CHARACTER

CHAPTER 16

HUMBLE

July 26, 2020

Dear Rosie, Dass, and Evangeline,

Today, we hiked Dogwood Canyon and took pictures. A picture of Rosie and Dass standing over a creek, a picture of Eva standing in a bald eagle's nest, and a picture of us all together. I love taking pictures with you girls and hanging them on the wall of the cabin. Sometimes I post pictures of us online.

Seems like everyone does this now. You girls live in a selfie culture. Just a few years ago, the selfie didn't even exist. When I was a boy, we had Polaroid pictures. (I'm not even going to try to explain how it worked.) But cameras faced forward, and you looked through the lens and took a picture. Something or someone else was the object. The camera was designed to look and shoot outward.

Now everyone has smartphones, and the camera lens can face you. You are the object. People take pictures of themselves and edit, filter, and post them online. Somehow this became normal. I wonder if, many years from now, children in history classes will ask their teachers, "Why did people take so many pictures of themselves?"

Some people live to take pictures of themselves, post them online, then soak up the attention. Attention feels good. But some people live for digital validation. They constantly check social media for any whiff of attention. Some post foolish, silly, or inappropriate pictures, hoping to "go viral." The temptation to achieve fame through social media is luring a generation to become YouTube or TikTok famous.

A *New York Times* article called "The Agony of Instagram" said the never-ending stream of fancy, well-curated images gives us Instagram envy. According to the article, these edited photos are a new form of torture: "Viewers . . . are expected to let the sumptuous photos wash over them and chip in with comments ('Gorgeous sunset!') and heart-shape 'likes,' which function as social currency, reinforcing the idea that every shot is a performance worthy of applause. The result is an online culture where the ethic is impress, rather than confess."

We, like Narcissus, are transfixed by our own reflections.

Don't do this. Don't live for attention. A person who does this is constantly asking for approval. And the act of constantly posting selfies comes across as self-absorbed. *Do you see me? Do you like me? Am I attractive? (Please click "like" if you think so.)*

There is something beautiful about humility, about thinking of others and being less self-centered and self-conscious. I think humility is quiet. It doesn't boast or strut or demand the spotlight. It moves from childish self-centeredness to others-centeredness. It doesn't walk around with a mirror duct-taped to its face. It sees others and considers. It listens. It is at peace.

Modesty and humility are cousins. Being modest means you don't brag, or grab credit, or bluster on about your success. Don't boast; you don't need to prove yourself to anyone. While others posture and climb for ranking, be secretly awesome. Focus on what you love and what you want to do, whether they like it or not. Dare to become great without telling anyone.

Ed is this way. He would rather deflect the conversation before talking too much about himself. He could brag about his cool job or the famous people he knows or any number of things. But he doesn't. My friend Scott is this way too. Whenever we talk, he's always asking me questions. I think conversations are like a game of catch: You throw the ball back and forth. You don't hog the ball. Scott is always passing it to others. He is genuine and concerned and caring and has many friends and open doors because of it.

All relationships need this kind of passing. No one wants to be in relationship with someone who is always all about themselves, someone who is a ball hog. I think humility is the basis of all our relationships with people and with God. All good things come from God. Knowing this allows us to see things the way they are. Humility is simply seeing things as they really are.

But our natural tendency is to believe we are the center of the universe. We experience all of life, our days and nights, our events and relationships through our personal filters and feelings. It is not natural for us to empathize or see things from someone else's perspective. We have to learn to do this. To share. To give. To listen. Some people never learn to move beyond themselves, to step down from their own pedestals.

I think humility has to do with ownership. It doesn't seek to make excuses or pass the blame; it owns faults, even when painful or humiliating. But pride is never wrong. It never apologizes. Never takes ownership. Pride leaves issues unresolved. Over time, the unresolved issues stack up like invisible bricks creating a wall between two people.

There is another type of pride, sneakier and harder to detect. It is not chest puffing and bragging, like Gaston in *Beauty and the Beast*. It is "victim pride."

When Adam was in trouble, he pointed at Eve and said, "It's not my fault!" When Eve was in trouble, she pointed at the snake and said, "It's not my fault!" I think the snake would have pointed at someone too, but there was no one left.

Children do this all the time. One is crying, and the adult approaches the other and asks, "Why did you hit him?" The child responds, "Because he pushed me." No. You were upset, so you decided to hit him. He did not make you do anything. You had a million options, but you chose to hit.

Today I was talking to a friend who was getting attacked with some accusatory and unfair texts. But the attacker was doing everything he was accusing her of doing! He was insisting it was not his fault and blaming her for his actions. It was confusing and ridiculous and maddening. So I sent this text back to my friend:

"We are all the hero of our own story."

Some people go to great lengths to remain the hero. No matter if the world disagrees with them, including all their friends. Some people fabricate a completely different reality to keep their position. They recruit friends who agree with them and reject the others, all to keep their hero status.

But I think humility and ownership and the acceptance of our need—our real need for Christ—pierces all that. When we finally accept we are finite and we fail and we need help, we are open to the possibility of God's grace and open to change.

Pride keeps us closed. And victim pride keeps us from taking ownership of our lives. When we are a victim who blames others, we don't need to apologize, because we were the one who was wronged. We are the one who needs an apology. The villain takes the role of the victim. Playing the victim allows us to blame others and tell our victim stories. Maybe we are hurt, but we do not look at ourselves or what we did or, in some cases, are still doing. Our victim stories keep our pride intact.

Victim pride has a double ego boost. The victim story is an emotional payoff because the person's ego remains intact by saying, "It's not my fault." This garnishes sympathy from others. And the second ego boost involves the victim posturing as an overcomer, standing up to rise against their feigned oppressors. *I am now overcoming what they did to me!*

Some people fabricate a new story where they can be the victim and never own their behavior. Anyone who disagrees will be evicted. Close friends are banished. Even family members are kicked out. This person may deny God or try to make God fit the victim narrative. The person who lives in victim pride cannot see their need for grace from God or anyone else.

Pride blames; it points the finger at someone else. But humility owns its faults; it does not blame. Humility is quick to take responsibility and ask forgiveness. Humility sees the truth, like the thief on the cross who said, "Jesus, remember me," or the man who prayed, "God, have mercy on me, a sinner." It knocks on the door of the Father's house and asks to come home.

Proverbs wisely says, "Humility comes before honor." There is nothing wrong with wanting honor, promotion, and recognition. But humility comes first and takes out the grasping. It also allows you to focus on your task at hand instead of worrying what others will think or say. Become great at your work, callings, and lives without needing to take endless selfies and show the world. Be great without needing anyone's validation. Own your mistakes. Even the bad ones. Especially those.

When you are humble, you are a bold contrast to a generation that desperately wants to be famous. They won't understand you. They won't understand why you don't brag and clamor for fame. Be humble anyway. Humility is such a rare and precious commodity that anyone who has it stands out in the crowd.

Be secretly awesome,
Dad

CHAPTER 17

KIND

July 29, 2020

Dear Rosie, Dass, and Evangeline,

When I was a boy, I watched *Mister Rogers' Neighborhood* every day. You girls used to watch Daniel Tiger. Daniel was born in Mr. Rogers' imagination. Mr. Rogers always treated his guests with kindness and empathy. As I watched him, it felt like we had a real relationship; he felt like a friend. His kindness traveled from his studio in Pittsburgh to Arkansas.

I wish you could have known your great-grandmother Helen. She was gentle and full of quiet joy. For her, kindness was a reflex. She never once raised her voice in anger or spoke negatively about anyone. When she needed to correct us, it was firm but soft. I can still hear her saying, "Oh no, honey, don't do that." I hope you girls are like her.

Kindness, like humility, is a way of being in the world. It is a way of relating to yourself and others. Kindness is not niceness, which tends to live on the surface. Some people act nice to get what they want. They may be nice because they want to sell you things or date you or get something from you. Niceness is outward; kindness is in the heart. Kindness has deep care and concern for the other.

It is full of grace and invitation. Kindness is an unspoken language. It says, "I am here and I am for you." Kindness is considerate. It considers others. It doesn't cut in line or push its way to the front. It is gentle and aware. It is not severe or harsh. Kindness builds bridges, creates trust, and makes easy friends.

I've been fortunate to spend time in Alaska. I went back a couple years ago and stayed with my friend Mike. We stayed off the grid on Kodiak Island, no cell phones or electricity, and hiked during the days. We hiked for miles and caught salmon and halibut and ate them every night.

One time, we were hiking about forty yards from a Kodiak bear as it was walking through a stream fishing for salmon. We were angling away from it to give it space as it fished. We were walking through five foot tall grass, watching the bear, when suddenly, three bear cubs stood up directly in front of me. Standing on their hind legs, looking at me, less than ten yards away. From somewhere behind them, I heard a loud, chuffing sound, deep throated and angry. Mama bear!

Because of the tall grass, we didn't even know they were there. And I had the strangest feeling, like when I went over the handlebars and flipped my bike, going full speed down the side of the mountain. My whole body tensed up and braced for impact. I knew it was gonna hurt, I was gonna break bones and maybe worse.

But just then, Mike spoke up. "It's okay. It's okay. We're sorry," he said in a loud but calm tone. Mike was carrying a .375 H&H rifle, but instead of shouldering it, getting ready to shoot, he was apologizing to mama bear. She kept making that angry sound; I was backpedaling slowly, trying to put some distance between me and certain death.

But Mike kept speaking kindly to her, and after a tense moment, the three cubs went down on all fours and, fortunately, ran back to her. Then they all ran off together. I don't know if Mike's kindness saved me from getting mauled or saved her from getting shot, but I'd like to think so. Animals respond to kindness. They respond to energy and nonverbal communication and can even read our faces.

Kindness is transcendent.

Several years ago, I had the honor to work and serve alongside people who were homeless. I remember the men who came to the shelter every day for food, clothes, or financial help. Most of them wore old clothes and slept outside in alleys and on grimy streets. Most had not bathed or shaved in weeks. Many had hard looks and narrow, suspicious eyes. They were survivors.

These men were not used to kindness. A few times, I had to break up fights as men argued about their place in line or who got the last gallon of frozen milk. All they owned were the clothes on their bodies and the worn-out shoes on their feet. Some had trash bags to hold their clothes.

Charlie, whom everyone called Two Hats, pushed around a metal grocery cart. Two Hats wore about six baseball caps at the same time and drew crosses all over his clothes in blue ink. When we first met him, Two Hats didn't speak to us. He only spoke to himself as he pushed his cart around the streets. Over time, Two Hats started opening up, and when we said hello to him, he smiled a big, toothless smile.

A few men who were once homeless helped me run the shelter. And sometimes Two Hats helped. I remember David, who talked in a loud voice. He was always giving me car advice: "Hey, John! Change that oil!" Carl was a rail-thin smoker. His frail body was wasting away in the final stages of a terminal illness.

We met thousands of people in the shelter. Many were desperate.

Many came from other cities and were transients. Some had mental and physical illnesses. Some needed a place to stay. Others were hungry or jobless and had unpaid bills or medical needs. All of them needed help. We helped with food and bills and clothing, but I think our most powerful gift was kindness. I watched kindness soften hard faces, comfort hurting people, and give them peace.

I remember one time watching Two Hats hand groceries to a homeless man who was afraid. Two Hats listened to him. The man started crying, and Two Hats hugged him. Kindness changed Two Hats, and now he passed his kindness on to others.

Kindness is contagious. It spreads from person to person. The British theologian Frederick William Faber wrote, "No kind action ever stopped with itself. . . . One kind action leads to another. . . . The single act of kindness throws out roots in all directions, and the roots spring up and make fresh trees. . . . This is the greatest work which kindness does to others,—that it makes them kind themselves."

Kindness transforms. Kindness changes people, and it changes us.

I hope you always stay kind,
Dad

CHAPTER 18
ENOUGH

August 1, 2020

Dear Rosie, Dass, and Evangeline,

Evangeline, we just had your birthday party. You told me you wanted purple cupcakes, so that's what we had. We sang. We blew out candles. You opened presents. The first one you opened was a Wonder Woman dress. You shrieked and put it on and wore it the rest of the day. You fought against imaginary villains and danced.

Last Christmas, you each had one giant present beside the tree. You shrieked and ran and tore into them so fast. One of you almost fell headfirst into the box! One year, I gave you giant teddy bears, and you laughed for a long time. I recorded it and sent your laughter to my friend Ryan, who put it in a song called "Four."

This year, you girls came to me with the idea of raising money for Burundi. Our church is building fifteen wells there to provide clean water. We have been fundraising, selling things to raise money for it. Books, workout gear, other items. As of today, we have raised six hundred dollars. I'm so grateful you girls decided to support the people of Burundi who need clean water. I'm proud of you for doing it. And it reminds me of Acts 20:35, which says, "It is more blessed to give than to receive."

This generosity is the opposite of all advertisements you see, those never-ending voices trying to persuade you: *Buy this! Need that! Buy now and save!* (Wait, what?) These voices are businesses that spend billions of dollars trying to convince you to buy their next new thing. Buy the new toy. Sparkly purse. Makeup set. You need more, so buy more. Buy this; become that. Consume the idol; become the idol. Buy the fancy purse; become a fancy woman. Buy your identity.

Don't buy it.

There is another lie hidden behind all those screaming voices: *You do not have enough, and because you do not have enough, you are not enough.* This is the great lie of our consumer culture: you are not enough. They say you are not enough until you have bought your identity. Then keep buying it, for the rest of your life.

Many young people today want to be famous. When they think about who they wish to become, their answer is simply, "Famous." The lure of fame promises attention. Significance. Fame seeking is the desire for approval and applause from others. This desire often asks the question, *Do you like me?* And a deeper one, *Am I enough?*

Fame seeking is the inevitable result of our consumer culture. It is the result of a culture that constantly tells us we do not have enough and we are not enough. When you seek fame, you give your power to others, you ask them to decide your worth. You submit to the crowd to decide your value. But the crowd is fickle and whimsical. Fame seeking is exhausting; you are always performing, always worrying what the crowd thinks. And it is a slippery place to build your lives.

But what if we stopped caring about their opinions?

What if we took our power back?

Others will say you are not enough until you have a romantic relationship. Our culture screams this lie at women. *If a man does not marry you, you are not enough.* As long as you stay single, you are incomplete, a half-person. So spend your life searching for a man; worry and scramble to secure a boyfriend and make him your husband. Then you will be complete, whole, and enough.

One lady told me, "I grew up hearing I needed a man, that I would never make it alone. I was told I needed a man to take care of me, to provide for me and financially help me make it through life. It was an unhealthy, wrong, and codependent message."

There is another problem with this lie—a man was never designed to complete you. Even a good and strong, kind and loving man. Even a man who spiritually leads you. Even a man who fights for you, romances you, protects and provides for you. If you grow up believing a man will make you complete, when you marry one, you will crash into a tidal wave of unmet expectations. You may feel disillusioned and unfairly blame him for not completing you.

Another lie you will hear is that your bodies are not enough. Others will try to tell you what is beautiful and what is not. Women hear this constantly. Wear these clothes. Curl your hair. Straighten your hair. Lose weight. Gain weight. Add muscle. Wear this makeup. Use this skin product. To be enough, you must constantly buy, change, and reinvent yourself.

Businesses will try to lay claim to your beauty, but you stand alone. Free from their false and greedy claims. You need none of their filters to shine. Some men will want you as objects of their desire. Your beauty is not an object to be captured, possessed by dirty hands. You owe them nothing; you don't need them to validate your beauty. Your beauty is priceless.

Another lie you may hear is that you are not religious enough.

Some people may try to use shame and guilt as a weapon against you. They say you must be this way or that way, or they remind you of your failures and tell you to get out. Some people try to be little judges to make little rulings and kick people out of their little clubs.

This judgmental spirit lives in what some people call cancel culture.

Cancel culture is the idea that when someone messes up, fails, or falls into sin, they should be canceled. Banished, eliminated, forgotten. Cancel culture uses shame to demean and discard them. Cancel culture is even found in the church, the place created for unconditional love, acceptance, and forgiveness.

The difference between cancel culture and accountability is that accountability seeks the good of the person, whereas cancel culture does not. Accountability comes from a kind place, a place of wanting someone to change, wanting the best for others. Cancel culture comes from a place of fear, control, and hate, masked as moral superiority.

Cancel culture promotes fear. When you are part of any community that cancels people, you cannot be honest with your own failures. There is no grace, no forgiveness. Only fear. You fear getting kicked out of the club, so you pretend everything is okay. You are forced to play the game. And it's tragic.

I know this is hard to talk about. Cancel culture is not a positive subject. I wish it didn't exist. I hope writing about this protects your hearts from those who try to use fear and shame to control you. The Bible tells us, "There is no fear in love." If you are ever afraid of anyone—a coach, a teacher, a family member, a friend, or someday, a boyfriend—it is not love. If anyone tries to use shame to control you, it is not love. Reject their lies. Sometimes it feels good to say no. Maybe practice saying it out loud right now. No. No. *No!*

Dass, this week you took your first voice lesson and sang "You

Say" by Lauren Daigle. You sang a line, and then Mrs. Terry sang. I sat in the corner of the cabin and pretended not to watch or listen. But my eyes teared up. It was beautiful to hear you sing that song, words that can be the foundation of your entire life. If you build your life on the truth of that song and by faith, you will never question your worth.

Always remind yourselves who you are and to whom you belong. Don't compare and compete. And remember, you don't need a bunch of things or a relationship to be enough. You are wonderfully made. You are the first one of your kind.

You are beautiful and enough,
Dad

CHAPTER 19

QUEEN

August 12, 2020

Dear Rosie, Dass, and Evangeline,

Names matter. Throughout your lives, you are called by the names your parents gave you on your birthday. There are millions of names in the world. Some have rich meanings or family meanings, some are beautiful sounding, some people grow into names or even change their names.

When you girls were born, we had specific names in mind. We envisioned:

Sahara Rose, the flower that blooms in the desert. *Rosie*.

Hadassah Ruth, the queen who saved her people. *Dass*.

Evangeline Love, the good news that saved the world. *Eva*.

In an earlier letter, we learned about brave women named Rose: Rosa Parks and Sister Rosemary Nyirumbe. We learned about a hero named Sophie who was part of the White Rose. This letter is about Hadassah, the orphan girl who became a queen who saved a nation.

Hadassah was raised by her cousin Mordecai after her parents died. He took her as his daughter and cared for her. The Hebrew name *Hadassah* means "myrtle flower," which is a symbol of hope. Maybe Mordecai called her Dass, Dassah, or Dassi when she was young.

Hadassah was exiled in a foreign country with the rest of her people, so she took on the Persian name Esther to hide her identity. She was lovely and beautiful. The Persian king was searching the nation for a queen. Scholars believe he was King Xerxes, the king who ruled over the kingdoms of Persia, Media, Babylon, everything from India to Ethiopia. He was the same king who invaded Sparta with two million soldiers.

After returning from his conquests, Xerxes searched his kingdom for a beautiful woman to marry. He was attracted to Esther more than any other woman. He chose her, set a crown on her head, married her, and made her his queen. Then he gave a great feast in her honor—Esther's feast—and the king proclaimed it a holiday.

Sometime later, a man named Haman became the king's adviser. He hated Esther's people, the Jews, so he manipulated the king into believing they were evil and should be killed. So the king, under Haman's guidance, issued a royal decree to have the Jewish people wiped out.

Mordecai learned of this death sentence and cried bitterly. Then he told Esther about the decree and said to her, "Do not think that because you are in the king's house you alone of all the Jews will escape. For if you remain silent at this time, relief and deliverance for the Jews will arise from another place, but you and your father's family will perish. And who knows but that you have come to your royal position for such a time as this?"

Mordecai knew that God would save his people, even if Esther stayed quiet and did not act. But he called her to step into her destiny and her name. This was her moment. She was an exile in a foreign land, with a foreign name, and married to a foreign king, but she was in the middle of God's timing and destiny for her life.

In that moment, Esther had a choice.

She could remain quiet and not reveal her identity as a Jew. From the outside, this looked like her best chance to live through the coming massacre. She could hide. But if she did that, her people, and Mordecai, would be destroyed. Or she could rise up. She could go to the king even though it meant risking her life. The king had disposed of the first queen, who did not obey. Maybe he would do the same to her.

After Esther heard Mordecai's bad news, she asked him to fast for her, to seek God on her behalf, for three days and nights. This was her first act. She said, "When this is done, I will go to the king, even though it is against the law. And if [I die], [I die]." She resolved to act, even if it meant her death.

Through Esther's actions and bravery, her nation was saved.

In your life, there may be times where nothing makes sense. There may be times when you feel like an exile, like you don't fit in. You may find yourself in the middle of some unspeakable tragedy or situation you never dreamed or wanted. But God sees you. And he is with you. Seek him. When the time is right and you are ready, he will call you to act.

These are divine moments. Moments when destiny collides with opportunity and need. This is your calling. Your calling is the work you are gifted and given to do. Calling is the thing you must do. As you girls grow into women, I hope you become like Queen Esther. There are some beautiful gifts from her life and story.

Esther submitted to the true King. She recognized that there was one greater than her husband, King Xerxes, the most powerful man alive. Her submission to this true King was her source of wisdom and bravery. Remember, no matter the situation, humility is always truth. A queen submits to the true King.

Esther was bold. By being bold and going directly to the king, she risked her life. She later risked her life again by revealing her identity as a Jew and standing up for her people. She stepped boldly into her calling and was willing to lay down her life for her people, which as John 15:13 says, is the greatest form of love. She did not fear death to save her people, and in this way, she was an early model of Christ, who gave his life for us. A queen is bold.

In your life, there will be transformational moments. Moments when you can take the easy way out, be silent when you should speak, or hide in fear. Moments when you are tempted to not think of others. There may be confusing or unfair moments; you may be placed in situations you never wanted or imagined. In these moments, I hope you see the greater story, like in the story of Esther. There is an Invisible Hand moving things around, moving people, arranging situations and events that you cannot see. In these moments, I hope you trust and rise up "for such a time as this."

You girls can lead nations and change the course of history.

> Always wear your invisible
> crowns,
> Dad

CHAPTER 20
WORDS

August 30, 2020

Dear Rosie, Dass, and Evangeline,

I can still remember and feel the kind words you have said to me. Moments you run to me and say things like, "I love you, Daddy. Thank you for getting us Shadow. Thank you for the bicycles." Your words make my heart smile, even now as I remember them. I can still hear your sweet voices. I hope you always speak life.

Words are a vehicle for love. Sometimes words stay with us for years, locked away like hidden treasures in our hearts. I can remember phrases, moments, times when people said good things to me, words of life and words about who I am in the world.

When I was four, on my first day of preschool, I remember Nana telling my teacher, "He is quiet but strong." When I was eight, I remember wrestling with my mentor, Sonny. His wife was worried about how hard we were wrestling, and he said, "This boy is tougher than an oak knot."

I remember getting a letter from your uncle Bill saying, "You are a man and a good man." It was the first time anyone had called me a man. I remember Wayne praying for me, saying I was like one of David's mighty men. I remember Scott telling me he was proud of me and the way I persevered through a hard situation.

These words became part of me. I still remember words and phrases people have spoken over me. Even as a little child. The two women who raised me always spoke life. They corrected me when needed but never berated me, guilt-tripped me, or raised their voices at me. They were gentle and good, and I was so blessed to have them.

Words can create and build; they can burn and destroy. Words build families. Words start friendships and wars. Words become part of us. Words are written in books and sung in songs; they are cried and prayed and spoken to God. Words are thoughts inside our own minds that shape what we believe about ourselves and the world.

Words speak light into the void of our doubts. Words create new dreams and visions. Words give us courage. Words dispel lies. Words fill our hearts, minds, and souls with good things. Words can even physically change our brains, bodies, and make us healthy. Jesus said, "A good man brings good things out of the good stored up in his heart, and an evil man brings evil things out of the evil stored up in his heart. [For out of the mouth, the heart speaks]."

If you have beauty in your hearts, it reflects in your speech, in the words you choose and the way you listen. Bullies are mean in their hearts before they ever say a word. Words are born in the mind and heart long before they are formed on the tongue. Learn to listen. You can learn a lot about someone by listening to them and by discerning intentions and feelings behind their words. You can learn their values. I think this is true of God too. His heart was displayed as he spoke you into being. You are his precious thought, formed in the well of his infinite affection.

Words are hearts spoken aloud.

The opposite is true too. Someone once said that the words you speak become the house you live in, and I think this is right. Words come out of the heart, and words go into the heart too. The words you speak make their way down from your mouths into your hearts and change you. So be careful what you say. In the Bible, James wrote,

A bit in the mouth of a horse controls the whole horse. A small rudder on a huge ship in the hands of a skilled captain sets a course in the face of the strongest winds. A word out of your mouth may seem of no account, but it can accomplish nearly anything—or destroy it!

It only takes a spark, remember, to set off a forest fire. A careless or wrongly placed word out of your mouth can do that. By our speech we can ruin the world, turn harmony to chaos, throw mud on a reputation, send the whole world up in smoke.

Your words are powerful. Choose them wisely.

The words you say about others, especially when they are not around, says a lot about your character.

As you get older, some teenagers will use curse words. I think they say them for the same reason they try nasty cigarettes or drinking: for approval. They may say these words pretending to be something they are not. But like cigarettes, curse words are full of toxins. Even when you are done smoking them, their toxic residue stays inside you. One cigarette won't change your lungs much, but if you are a chain smoker, your lungs will become black and shriveled. I think curse words have the power to blacken your heart.

Measure your words. Be mindful of what you say. A patient, thoughtful response is far better than blurting out thoughts and feelings or interrupting and talking over others. Someday you will see this on Twitter, or whatever social media site people use when you are older. Everyone on Twitter is talking and shouting and reacting, and it seems like no one is listening. Don't do this. Don't impulsively react with your words and talk over other people online or in person. Sometimes men do this; people call it "mansplaining." (Women can do it, too, but for some reason, some men have this compulsive tendency.)

Remember, it's fine if you don't respond to someone immediately. Even when you have strong feelings and ten thousand things to say. It may even be best to sleep on it and respond in the next few days. I think the most powerful words are spoken into silence. Instead of throwing words into a scrambled pile of other words, listen first, then speak with intention, wisdom, and conviction.

Listen first. Don't form your answers in your minds. Don't be an opinion waiting to share. People usually don't need or want solutions; they just want to be heard. Once a person feels heard, they feel known and loved and often find the solution themselves.

Your words will echo in hearts for decades and generations. Kind words from my grandmother still live in me, and she passed some twenty years ago. I'm sure kind words from her grandmother lived in her too. Generations will be impacted by what you say.

Always speak life,
Dad

PART 6

FRIENDS AND RELATIONSHIPS

CHAPTER 21

FRIENDS

September 1, 2020

Dear Rosie, Dass, and Evangeline,

You girls have something special. You have one another.

I know sometimes it doesn't feel that way. Sometimes siblings get annoyed or fight or complain or compete. As you grow, friends will come and go and move away. But the three of you will always have one another. And I hope you understand how special this is. Stay kind and loyal, and cheer for each other.

You girls are sisters, and I hope you always stay close friends.

Many siblings are rivals. They compete with one another; they bicker and stew and fight. They argue and complain and pick at one another. Siblings who are jealous rivals miss out. They miss out on the gift of friendship and the potential to make each other better. They don't realize friends can help achieve what they want in life. And if you girls are friends instead of rivals, there are no limits in what you can achieve.

A rival is against you. But a friend is for you and with you.

I hope you girls are friends and not rivals. Having a friend means you don't go through life alone. A friend is someone to give you high fives when you score a soccer goal, someone who picks you up when you fall. A friend cheers for you when you need it and cries with you when you need it. They show up for you and know you; they know all your good, your faults and failures, and still accept you. They know when to be quiet and when to speak the truth. A friend is someone who believes in you even if you no longer believe in yourself.

A friend is someone we trust and allow into our lives. A friend is someone we let into the deep and tender places, and a friend walks gently there. We were all created for friends and community. None of us can grow into our best selves without friends. None of us reaches our destiny alone.

Friends help us become who we were born to be.

I'm convinced none of us see ourselves as we are. Most people go through life having no idea how others perceive them. Most people judge themselves by their own intentions and ideas that others never see. If we have good intentions toward others, we think we are good people. But this is not always the case.

I know a man who is always nice to me. If you met him, you'd think he's nice too. We were hanging out a few months ago, and I had some great news to tell him. But every time our conversation slowed down, he kept talking. Every single time I tried to speak, he launched into another story. So for two hours I sat there, listening to him.

It's good to listen. Sometimes friends need us to listen. Sometimes we need them to listen too. But he never stopped talking, never took a breath, never passed the ball of the conversation. I ended up leaving without sharing anything at all. My conversations with him are almost always this way. Frustrating.

If you asked him, he would think it was a good exchange. His intentions were good. He was happy to see me. He didn't realize he railroaded the entire conversation. I'm sure he was not aware that he didn't ask a question or give me a chance to speak. I have had other similar interactions with him, where he was unaware of himself. He doesn't have bad intentions; he just doesn't see.

A friend helps us see ourselves.

To see yourselves, go to a trusted friend, someone you know and respect. Ask them, "What do you think?" Then patiently listen. Allowing someone else to reflect back onto us requires openness and humility. Someone who is proud does not allow this. Therefore, the proudest people often do not see themselves.

I'm grateful to have a few good friends. It's good to be friendly to everyone, but wise people have a small friend circle. Good friends, deep friends, take time to grow and develop. Trust takes time. Getting to know someone takes time. Finding someone with the same values as you, someone who is loyal and good and kind, well, those kinds of people are rare.

Many people stay home and wish for friends. They want to be included and get invited to parties or functions, connect with others and have friends. But they wait for friends to come to them. They may even be sad, thinking, *I don't have many friends.* Don't wait for others to reach out to you. Pursue friends.

Here's a friend secret: *be a friend initiator.*

In most of my relationships, I am the pursuer. This means I don't wait for others to reach out to me. I am the one who texts first, who remembers birthdays, encourages, recognizes and celebrates milestones, and tries to stay in touch. By taking initiative, I have built many deep friendships. By being the initiator, I am not passive or sad or wishing I had friends. I do something about it.

Sometimes friends move away. Some stop texting back. Life

changes. This can be sad. But if you are always the only one texting, the only one pursuing or reaching out, the friendship is not mutual. Some people only want to be in your life if you are pursuing them. Some people want you to flatter and smile and agree with them. But that's not a friendship; it's more of a fanship. Don't be a fan or beg or grovel for people to be your friends. You are worth more than that.

Here's another friend secret: *be an encourager.*

If you set your hearts to be encouragers, you are less likely to grow discouraged when people don't respond. When you're an encourager, you don't reach out hoping to win the "best friend" position. You are not trying to control or gain or get anything from them. You are taking a genuine interest in them and their lives. Reach out to encourage people, to listen to, care for, and serve them in this way. Then you are not expecting anything in return.

Set the posture of your heart to give, and it will always be full. You have needs, emotional and otherwise. We all do. But don't lead with your need for friendship. Lead with love. Then, when someone responds, you have the foundation for a genuine friendship.

A friend is loyal; she is for you and has your best interests in mind. She won't betray the things you share in confidence; she won't bad-mouth you when you are not around. She knows how to keep her word. It takes trust and time to build a friendship, and it happens when two people open up slowly over time.

Good friends listen patiently. They keep passing the ball in the conversation. They take a breath. They hold space for you. They are wise and kind. They value you; they want to know more about you and respect you and what you have to say.

Here is one more friend secret: *be the kind of friend you want in your life.*

Be all those good things you want, and you will attract like-minded friends. You often see like-minded people flock together. (Remember the letters on being thankful, humble, and kind; they are a good start.) Be that person and look for those friends who call you to be your best self. Those friends are the keepers.

You girls are keepers,
Dad

CHAPTER 22
BOUNDARIES

September 15, 2020

Dear Rosie, Dass, and Evangeline,

There is a word I wish I knew when I was your age. That word is *boundaries*.

It would have helped me a lot, especially in high school and college. When I was in high school, I worried about what people thought of me. Most people do this to some extent. But I was a people pleaser. I had a hard time saying no. It was like I was waiting for others to decide what they liked and would accept. Like a chameleon, I adapted in different rooms to blend in. I rarely spoke out or gave my full opinion. I did not take up my space in the room. Over time, I grew so used to pleasing others, I forgot who I was.

When you do this, it feels like you are a show pony. Make them happy. Prance around. Be funny. Don't disagree. Just smile and nod. The thing is, when you set your hearts on pleasing others, you are passive and let other people run your lives. I did this. I was worried if I had edges and opinions, I'd lose relationships. So I stayed quiet. Or

I tried to be the funny guy. I used to think I was being popular, but I was living in fear.

I had no boundaries because I was so worried about acceptance. Dr. Henry Cloud and Dr. John Townsend wrote a book about boundaries that I highly recommend. They wrote, "Boundaries define what is me and what is not me. A boundary shows where each individual ends and someone else begins, leading each person to a sense of ownership and responsibility. . . . Knowing what we are to own and take responsibility for gives us freedom."

In high school, I did not know where I ended and someone else began. All my lines were blurry. Boundaries have to do with our values, what we will accept and not accept. This comes from knowing who we are. When you know who you are, you don't need to dance or strive for acceptance. You can create boundaries that stem from your values, boundaries that help you make decisions in your lives and relationships.

Boundaries are our set of expectations we take into relationships. They are rules about who and what behavior we will accept and not accept. Here is an example:

I never allow anyone to scream at me, which can be verbal abuse. I never allow anyone to push me, touch me inappropriately, or hit me, which can be physical abuse. When someone tries to do these things, or threatens to do these things, I will keep my boundary and not allow it. If they do them anyway, I will make sure it never happens again, which probably means permanently ending the relationship.

Boundaries help keep the good in and the bad out. Setting boundaries involves taking responsibility for our choices. Boundaries help you stay out of toxic relationships and know when to part ways with someone. Boundaries are sacred agreements you make and keep with yourselves.

Boundaries test the quality of our relationships. The people in our lives who respect our boundaries will appreciate our opinions. But those who don't respect our boundaries are telling us they don't love our nos. They only love our yeses, our compliance. It's as if they are saying, "I only like you when you do what I want."

The other night, I was standing in line at a gas station, waiting to check out. The lady in front of me was telling the attendant about her relationship. From what she was saying, it sounded dreary. "Yeah, he just got out of prison again. He is angry. Yells at me all the time. The other night, he came home and was yelling and breaking things in the house, so I left for the night." Then she said, "He's been like this for years. I know he won't ever change."

It made me sad for her. I was frustrated because I felt like I couldn't help. I wish I'd said something compassionate and full of empathy. Compassion is always a good starting place.

I would have said something like, "Hello, ma'am. I couldn't help but overhear what you were saying. I'm terribly sorry you are being treated that way. No one should ever treat you like that. No one should ever yell or scream at you and make you afraid. No one should drive you out of the house the way he does. It is awful. And I'm sorry for the fear you feel, the disruptions and chaos he brings into your relationship, life, and home."

Then I would have said, "I want to tell you something else. What you allow will continue to happen. If you allow this man to act this way, he will probably continue to do so. I may even come back into this gas station in five years, and you could be standing in this same line, telling this same story to this same attendant, this story about this man who forces you out of your own house. Until you refuse to be treated this way, it may happen for the rest of your life.

"I hope this doesn't sound cruel or sound like bad news. It's not.

It's just the opposite. Sometimes fear makes us feel we are powerless. Fear makes us feel like we cannot change our lives and our circumstances, and we are doomed to accept them, no matter how dire. You are not powerless. You are strong enough to stand and change this situation.

"But because you have been beaten down for years, you don't feel strong. You don't see your worth anymore. You are worth more than this. I hope if I see you in here, five years from now, you have an entirely different life. A life where you are not afraid, where you no longer live with a bully, where you have hope and joy again. Even though you don't feel like it right now, you have the power to stand up and change it."

When someone disrespects you and steps over your boundary, it is critical to stand up for yourself and say no, even if it means losing the relationship. Sometimes you may need to change your friends and your environment. The hardest part about boundaries is having the self-respect to keep them. When that happens, I hope something fierce rises up in you and says, *No. I will not allow someone to cross my boundaries and trample my worth. I will stand up for myself and what I know is right.*

You will meet many people who test, push, and disrespect you and try to violate your boundaries. Especially as women. You will meet "mansplainers"—men who talk over you, talk down to you, and talk louder than you. Some men assume they are better, stronger, smarter, more competent or talented than you, just because you are a woman. This is sexism and a shame. Because of their ignorance, they miss out on friendships with brave, smart, and strong women like you.

Some friends will try to pressure you into making bad choices. They want you to make bad choices with them, so they push you into doing things you know you should not do. Many people go along with the pressure because they want to be popular and don't want to lose friends.

If your friendship relies on you making bad choices, like drinking or doing drugs or being pressured into something physical, it is not a real friendship. A real friend will not try to push you into anything you don't want to do. A real friend respects your choices. When anyone pressures you, remember your no and add "goodbye."

You will gain and lose friends. You may lose some whom you love dearly. Some friends will move away or go to another school or city or town. Some friends will hurt you or betray you or use you. Some friends may try to cancel you, like the older brother from the story of the lost son. But you will recover. You will heal. And there is beauty in every friendship and wisdom hidden in the losses.

There is some work you need to do when you set boundaries. You have to ask, *Who am I? What do I value? What do I expect in relationships and my life? What will I not tolerate? What will I bring into relationships?*

I have talked with you girls about identity and belonging. We have talked about who you want to become. Something else that helps us set boundaries is our constant. Your constant is the person by whom you should measure all your relationships. You may even have a few constants. Think of the good people in your life. Who has loved you with kindness? Who has cared for you and wanted the best for you? Those people are your constants.

Relationships can be confusing. Sometimes we get so caught up in our emotions, it's hard to make a rational decision. And some people are good at manipulation and deception and twisting your emotions. Some people just want to use you. When you are not sure about a relationship, when someone is making you feel confused or upset, think about your constant. This will give you wisdom. Ask yourselves, *Would my constant treat me this way?* If the answer is no, then close the door.

Your constant helps you define your own boundaries. Bring those expectations into your relationships. Remembering your constant will help you set boundaries and give you strength to keep them. When things get hard, ask, *How would my constant behave? Would my constant do this to me?*

Speak up and stand out. Don't shrink back. Don't play small. Don't let others silence you or push you into who they think you should be. Be you. Be fully you.

Be you and keep your boundaries,
Dad

CHAPTER 23
SPIRITUAL FAMILY

September 22, 2020

Dear Rosie, Dass, and Evangeline,

I remember dressing up for Sunday morning church. White button-down shirts and penny loafers and a tan sweater vest. We went to St. James. It was near the "ninja park" that you and I used to go to sometimes. St. James had classes before the service, called Sunday school. I know, I know, it sounds dreadful, but it was actually pretty fun. We had parties for the holidays. I remember this one game called a cakewalk. If you were standing on the right number when the music stopped, you won a cake! I thought that was pretty cool. I don't remember much from church, but I knew I was loved.

Years later, my friend Jon, the same one from college, told me he was starting a church and asked if I wanted to help. He wanted to start one downtown and meet in a restaurant or a bar. I had never started a church before, but I trusted Jon, so I said yes.

On Tuesday nights, a group of us started meeting at his downtown loft. Chad, Amy, Barb, Dustin, Angie, Larry, Chuck, Amanda, and a few others. Jon said he felt like we were supposed to pray before we did anything, before we tried to have church services. So we prayed for one another, for the city, for the people around us.

I remember one time, in the middle of prayer, I peeked. (I don't know who created the "heads down, eyes closed" prayer rule or even if it should be a rule.) I remember looking up and seeing Chuck with his hand on the window. At first, I didn't know what he was doing, then I realized he was praying. He was praying for the city. He had this intense look on his face, like deep concern, like when someone is telling you heavy or hard news. He cared. I knew Chuck well enough to know it was not a show. He prayed, and he cared. Everyone cared.

I think when you pray for someone, it is the purest form of love. You are thinking the best thoughts for them. You are hoping and believing and asking God for the best. I believe God hears us, and I believe, when we pray, it changes us too. I think the best prayers are the simple ones. *Please. Thank you. I love you. Help.*

We sang together. Jon had a Bible verse he read often. From the prophet Isaiah, chapter 61. He named our Tuesday nights "61." The chapter talks about having "beauty instead of ashes," "joy instead of mourning," and "praise instead of a spirit of despair." Isaiah said,

> They will be called oaks of righteousness,
>   a planting of the LORD
>   for the display of his splendor.
>
> They will rebuild the ancient ruins
>   and restore the places long devastated;
>   they will renew the ruined cities.

Isaiah wrote this chapter to a people in exile. They had been taken, their cities left in ruins. Hundreds of years later, Jesus quoted the first part of this chapter, as he was the fulfillment of Isaiah's prophecy. Some two thousand years later, we held it up in prayers for our city. We prayed for beauty, joy, praise, and restoration for people. As we prayed, things happened. Other people joined us too. People found restoration and healing.

This was a special and supernatural time. A full-heart moment. My friends were glad to see me. Everyone smiled and said, "John!" Everyone hugged me and respected me and loved me. I loved them too. Every Tuesday night felt like walking into a birthday party. We celebrated and loved one another. And it was bigger than all of us, our prayers for one another and for the city knitted us all together. We were family.

I used to think church was a place to go on Sunday mornings. Now I know church is a family we belong to every day.

Years later, I joined another spiritual family in Portland, Oregon. It was led by my friend Duke. He and his wife, Caroline, invited people into their home. Duke had this long lumberjack beard and wore a plaid shirt and the same flip-side hat every day. I don't think I ever saw Duke without it. He is humble, sharp, and a deep thinker. He's one of the best men I know. At his house, we had dinner, then someone shared a personal story. We were honest about our faults and accepting of one another. Duke taught the Bible by asking questions. We prayed. We became family.

I asked Duke why he thought our group was special, and he said, "We had to play it honest. Portland people don't really go to church on Sunday mornings. They don't do attractional church. Meaning, make a cool church service, with lights and singing and attract people to come. They just don't go. We met in living rooms and around the dinner table."

Duke continued, "Most people go to church and listen and go

home. But just information, just left-brain content, falls flat when it comes to human transformation. If people don't have an experience of joy and loving attachment, secure identity and deep community (even correcting community), they don't mature in Christ. Impersonal, anonymous church is a fool's errand."

I hope you girls find a spiritual family. It takes longer to find a spiritual family than it does a building. So be patient. Keep looking. I hope you find a spiritual family who shows up for you and loves you. A family who celebrates you or cries with you when you need, who prays with you and always believes the best for you.

I love you and am praying for you,
Dad

PART 7

FINDING AND BEING IN LOVE

CHAPTER 24

LOVE AS BEING

September 29, 2020

Dear Rosie, Dass, and Evangeline,

Being your dad has taught me a lot about love. I remember the nights after you girls were born, I was filled with fierce and loving protection. I would protect you at all costs. I patiently fed you every night after midnight, determined to make sure you were cared for and loved. I spent many hours watching you sleep, your tiny chests rising and falling.

Love came to me as a grace, a gift. Love wasn't something I had to reach for or muster or create; it just came. Even though you girls could not speak, you understood the tones of words and facial expressions. You communicated with smiles when you were happy, cries when you were hungry, and rubbing your hands on your faces when you were tired. A few weeks in, you could laugh. From early on, you girls recognized love and knew how to give and receive it.

Love is a way of being.

Love is a way of interacting with others. Love is hard to define. But I think love is warm. It is not cold to the touch. Not callous. Not objective when another heart is broken or sad or suffering. Love is moved with compassion. Love cares.

Jesus told a story about a man who was ambushed, robbed, and left dying in a ditch. He was in trouble and needed help. A preacher walked by on his way to church, too busy to help. He saw the dying man but clutched his Bible to his chest and kept going. Then another religious man came by, but when he saw the dying man, he pretended to look at his phone and kept walking.

Finally, a third man came. He wasn't special or privileged. But when he saw the dying man, his heart was filled with compassion. He stopped, called 911, and did everything he could to make sure the man would stay alive. After that, he paid for the man to stay in a hotel while he recovered.

After telling this story, Jesus asked, "Which of these three do you think was a neighbor?"

The religious leaders answered him, "The one who had mercy on him."

Jesus replied, "Go and do likewise."

Our friend Bob did something like this. You can read this story in his book *Everybody Always,* which is one of my favorites. When Bob found out his next-door neighbor and friend, Carol, was dying, he wanted her to know she was not alone. So he bought two walkie-talkies and told her, "Call me anytime." For the rest of her life, Bob checked on her, making sure she had everything she needed. Her favorite hot dogs. Balloons. A front-row seat to the neighborhood parade.

Bob said, "There's no school to learn how to love your neighbor, just the house next door. . . . Each of us is surrounded every day by our neighbors. They're ahead of us, behind us, on each side of us. . . . It's one thing we all have in common: we're all somebody's neighbor, and they're ours. This has been God's simple yet brilliant master plan from the beginning. He made a whole world of neighbors. We call it earth, but God just calls it a really big neighborhood."

Love is not indifferent. Love sees. Love cares.

When you lose your ability to care, you lose the thing that makes you human: your heart. And that is a scary thing. Some of the worst deeds in history were done by people who lost heart, by people who stopped caring. They were able to do horrible things because they no longer felt love or sadness or compassion.

When you lose your heart, you lose yourself.

We see this lostness all the time. We see the opposites of love. Words can be loving, and love can be expressed through words, but words are not love. Actions are love. Someday, when you're older, boys will tell you they love you, hoping to use it as a magical phrase to grasp you and use you. But remember, love is not measured by words but by actions. Believe actions, not words.

Love does not punish. It does not hurt back. Some people use fear and pain as a consequence. They believe, *You hurt me, so I will hurt you back*, or, *You didn't do what I wanted, so now you must pay*. But in your relationships with friends or someday a boyfriend, punishment doesn't correct a person; it just teaches them how to be afraid. And there is no fear in love.

Love does not undermine. Some people gossip and cut others down. Gossip is talking bad about another person behind their back. It doesn't hurt us physically, but it may be more damaging than a punch. Some people tear others down and then smile and act kind to their face. Gossip is mean and wrong. I hope you never do this. And if your friends gossip a lot, find new friends.

We see examples of un-love all the time. Drivers shake their fists and yell, "Learn how to drive!" Internet people hurriedly type, "I am outraged!" Offense culture is the latest fashion.

Paul described love in 1 Corinthians 13 when he wrote,

Love is patient, love is kind. It does not envy, it does not boast, it is not proud. It does not dishonor others, it is not self-seeking, it is not easily angered, it keeps no record of wrongs. Love does not delight in evil but rejoices with the truth. It always protects, always trusts, always hopes, always perseveres.

Love never fails.

This is a verse you see everywhere. When I read it, it kind of reminds me of those pictures people buy at Target. You know, those flowy-cursive ones, the ones you post on Instagram or hang in your living room and drink hot chocolate and read, holding the warm mug in your hands. *Ahh. Makes me feel better about myself.*

But I don't think this verse is supposed to be read that way. I don't think it's supposed to be read at all. I think this verse is supposed to read you. When I see this verse as a mirror, it reads me and makes me ask myself,

Am I this way? Am I patient? Am I kind, or am I short with people? Do I envy others and want what they have? Do I compare and grab? Am I gracious, or am I rude? Do I give my full attention to everyone, or do I overlook those who I don't see as valuable or cool? Do I seek the good of others? Do I love freely, without control or manipulation, or do I try to use people as objects of my desire? Am I easily irritated? Do I hold on to past hurts, keeping a list of wrongs? Do I rehearse someone's failures over and over again, or do I forgive? Am I protective of others and trusting? Do I hope for and fight for the best?

When I look at myself in the mirror of Scripture, I am both

encouraged and convicted. I think it's supposed to be this way. The mirror shows us how to move closer to love. It shows us our need for grace, and it encourages us to pray and seek to become these things. As Bob said, "We'll become in our lives what we do with our love."

> Keep becoming love,
> Dad

CHAPTER 25

LOVE AS KNOWING

October 10, 2020

Dear Rosie, Dass, and Evangeline,

I didn't know you before you were born. I loved you before we met, but I didn't know you yet. From the moment I met you, I started learning all about you. What you looked like. Your sweet voices and personalities. When you were born, I started seeing you and loving your uniqueness. And I am still learning and knowing you.

Love is a way of being. Love is also a way of knowing.

Love has to do with knowing and seeing another person. This has to do with intimacy. It has been said that "intimacy" is like saying "into me see." Love is seeing into another person, their deep places, and accepting them.

Love requires opening up. This happens slowly over time. This intimate, mutual knowing is the requirement for deep love. The opposite of this knowing is fear, or shame. Adam and Eve tried to hide from God in their shame by making clothes and covering themselves. Many adults hide too. They worry about what others think and hide behind fancy jobs and cars and houses. They hide behind identities and personalities they have crafted and polished. They hide behind online personas that are filtered and curated to reflect their best days, their best angles, their best selves. I'd like to see a social media account that is unfiltered. Bad hair days. Flat tires. Rainy skies. Ugly plates of food. Confessions about things that didn't work out. It's hard to know someone when they always hide their struggles and only show the good.

When children are young, they don't try to hide as much. Maybe they hide when they sneak an extra cookie or something. But I think young children are not very good at hiding yet. And that's a beautiful, beautiful thing. All three of you girls are this way. Eva, I love watching how unfiltered you are. You don't mask your feelings. You shriek for joy and hug and smile and laugh from your soul. When you are sad, you cry. When you miss me, you tell me. You are fearless with your heart, and it is radiant and beautiful and inspiring. It reminds me of something I once had, something I hope to find again.

Intimacy requires an unfiltered life.

Intimacy requires courage. And intimate knowing is the opposite of infatuation. Infatuation creates a strong, emotional attachment, maybe obsession, with a person we don't know. Infatuations are one-sided and often mistaken for love. And the Latin word for *infatuation* means "to make foolish."

Some people say they love songs or sunsets, a movie or a person they see across the room for the first time. These emotions and attractions are powerful. But it is probably best to call these feelings appreciation instead of love.

Every few years, a boy band comes along, dressed in the latest fashions, with tousled hair and high-pitched voices. They sing and strut around onstage, while millions of screaming girls go to the concerts, cry, and get hysterical. The girls obsess over the boys and hang posters on their walls at home. The girls insist they love these strutting boys. But the girls don't know them, and the boys don't know the girls either. There is no mutual knowing. No intimacy. The girls are just infatuated members of a fan club.

Many people enter relationships this same way, especially romantic relationships. They see someone they admire, have an emotional or physical attraction, and decide they are "in love" with a person with zero knowledge about them. It's like Anna in the movie *Frozen*. She says yes to a marriage proposal minutes after meeting Hans—without even knowing his last name! She dreams about romance as "a chance to change my lonely world."

But Anna does not know anything about Hans. She doesn't know he is a liar and wants to use her to gain power. She does not know his values, his character, his heart. She doesn't know his family. She has no intimate knowledge of him. (And not much surface knowledge either.) In the end, Hans is a traitor and, with the opportunity, maybe even a murderer. Anna's loneliness and desperation caused her to make a foolish decision, and it nearly cost her everything.

There are two extremes here. There is one who acts foolish, throwing herself at anyone who shows her attention. Like Anna. And there is one who never gives love a chance. Like Elsa. They "conceal, don't feel, don't let them know." Elsa hides in fear. While her heart will not get broken, it will eventually freeze. The closed-off heart hides away in fear. The oversharing heart is desperate and needy.

There are many who make foolish relationship decisions. Even adults do this boy-band kind of dating and rush into marriages, like Anna. People often get married without knowing the other person, believing them to be someone they are not. These people make impulsive and emotional decisions that leave them hurting and disillusioned in the end.

Other people live in fear and never open up. These people usually have been hurt and scarred by others. Betrayal and broken hearts introduce pain and fear. Trusting others can be hard to do again after heartbreak. It may feel impossible to open up again. In *The Four Loves*, C. S. Lewis wrote, "To love at all is to be vulnerable."

Opening up to other people creates space for love. Even friendship requires us to share ourselves with others, to take the risk of trust. Many people call this risk being vulnerable. Vulnerability is the birthplace of love.

But instead of being vulnerable, many people hide and wear masks, pretending to be something they are not. This is part of the tragedy of the fall.

Adam and Eve disobeyed and tried to hide from God. They had one command to follow. When they broke it, they tried hiding behind clothes and excuses. They blamed each other. They knew shame for the first time, and it separated them from relationship. Before, they were naked and not ashamed. Before, they walked with God in the garden. After they sinned, they hid from God. Their shame was a barrier to love.

Love calls us out of hiding. Love calls us to be brave and vulnerable and present. Love is built slowly over time, with mutual intimate knowledge and trust. I have talked with you girls about the difference between intimacy and infatuation. Don't fall for a smooth-talking Hans. Be patient. Take the time to build loving relationships.

I love knowing you,
Dad

CHAPTER 26

ROMANTIC LOVE

October 21, 2020

Dear Rosie, Dass, and Evangeline,

You girls can love now; you can love as young girls and teenagers. Children often love with more purity, more hope, than adults. Evangeline, today you kept running up and kissing me on the cheek and then running away again. If the whole world loved each other like you girls love me, it would be a far better and brighter place.

There is a love that is side by side: friendship. And there is a love that is face-to-face: romantic love. This face-to-face, romantic love is a weighty thing. It requires more than youthful idealism or hope. It needs maturity. Caution. Wisdom. Pacing. And the gift of time. Romantic love is not for the faint of heart. It is not for the frivolous or reckless.

The wise route is for you to wait, grow, and learn who you are as women before offering your hearts to anyone. It helps to know yourselves and what you want and need before walking out onto the treacherous path of love. In a few years, these words may sound frustrating to you. The boys will come around, showering you with flowers and compliments and attention. Right now, the boys your age are awkward and don't know how to act. Some of them pick on you or make fun of you. They may like you but don't know how to tell you yet. But they will learn.

They will learn to give you attention and say things like, "You are pretty." This attention feels good, especially if it is from a boy you like or think is cute. You girls are pretty. So you will hear that from boys. But it's in these emotional, feel-good moments when you must keep your hearts tethered to the shore. Don't rush and let yourself fly away into the clouds, like Anna, saying, "I'm in love!" Remember, love requires time and knowledge.

You are wise to wait until you are an adult before giving anyone your heart. I am writing this letter to the future you, to be read many years from now. With that said and all the proper cautions in place, let's explore this beautiful, treacherous thing.

Your first experience of romantic love may be unsettling. Your attraction to a boy may consume your thoughts and emotions. You may lose sleep. You may forget to eat. (Please remember to eat and sleep.) Romantic love is a beautiful upheaval. Adrienne Rich said it is "a process, delicate, violent, often terrifying to both persons involved."

Remember, there is a love that befriends and a love that beholds. There is a love that is side by side and a love that is face-to-face. Friendship is side by side, friends walking together with a common purpose. Friends are loyal, and they are for each other. Romantic love is face-to-face, appreciating and beholding. The strongest relationships and marriages are a combination of both.

Romantic love is seeing and allowing yourself to be seen. This love is freedom, not fear. Trust, not blame. This love leads to attraction and enchantment with its wildness and longing. This love is naked and not ashamed. In Song of Solomon, we see distance and nearness, appreciation and pursuit of a romantic partner. Romantic love sees you for you, accepts you, and loves all of you and all your pieces.

Psychologist Arthur Aron believed two complete strangers could love each other if they opened up and saw each other. So he conducted an experiment. He asked strangers to sit face-to-face and ask each other increasingly personal questions. These questions started simple, then got more intimate. Six months later, one pair was married.

Friendship and romantic love are not at war with each other. The seeing informs the serving. You think, *I see him better, so I know how to better serve him. I understand who he is, which allows me to be a better friend and walk beside him.* And the friendship may turn into admiration, into romance, longing, attraction, and commitment.

When a couple is together for a long time, the responsibilities, mortgages, activities, and jobs often pile on. Many couples stop looking at each other, stop romance, and focus on the tasks at hand. They work together as side-by-side partners. This teamwork is good and necessary. But many couples who work well as side-by-side partners forget how to see each other face-to-face. They stop beholding, stop appreciating, stop seeing.

When the flurry of activity settles, these couples may wake up and feel disillusioned, remembering what romantic love used to feel like. Many accept their side-by-side partnership as their new reality. Others give up, feeling like romantic love can never return. They don't understand that their posture toward each other has changed.

Even though their feelings are real and their relationship feels like it has lost something, any couple can learn to change their posture. They can learn to see each other again. They can find the joy of rediscovery. Remember, love is more powerful than feelings. Feelings do not have the final say over our relationships.

Face-to-face love is curiosity, attention, adoration, and appreciation, not control. This appreciation is freely given; it is not manipulative. It is not a means to an end, and it requires nothing back from you. Romantic love is not *I did this, so you should respond.* You are free to accept or not accept their gift. You are free to decline. And if your declining invokes a tantrum, an emotional fit, or guilt trip, be grateful that you declined. Any man worthy of you won't do these childish things.

Love is not childish or needy. Some men are needy and want to emotionally tie themselves to you, depending on you almost like a mother. Most of them don't even know this. C. S. Lewis wrote, "Need-love says of a woman 'I cannot live without her.'" But need love is the opposite of romantic love and even friendship love. Need love cannot give comfort, happiness, protection. It doesn't look to give anything at all. It only wants to feed.

One book that has taught me about face-to-face love is *The 5 Love Languages* by Gary Chapman. It showed me the languages of intimacy and how to connect, and taught me how to love better. In the book, Chapman identified five languages of the heart: gifts, quality time, words of affirmation, meaningful touch, and acts of service. Most of the time, we give and receive love in these ways.

Words are my love language; they are the way I feel most loved. Maybe this is why letters connect with me. Maybe this is why I'm writing a book of letters to you.

The way we receive love is the way we normally give it to others. So if words make me feel loved, then I assume others want to hear kind, loving words. I spend time speaking kind words and writing texts and letters. But to love another person, I must learn *their* love language, how they communicate and feel loved.

One day, you girls will learn your love languages and how to identify the love languages of others. And one day, in the distant future, you can come back to this letter and read it when you want to know more about romantic love.

I love you,
Dad

———————

Love will last
through journey's pass
through dark swallows of night
through dawn's breaking light
through the long shadow of the fall.
Love will last
when weary days retire
when tempest pounds and autumn leaves expire
when spring greens shine and beam
when life peeks forward and blossoms in the
    trees.
Love will last
through days and months and years
through the fierce gaze of lovers and through
    their tears
through joy and pain and songs of immortal and
    divine things
until the Great Feast beckons and calls us home.
   —"LOVE WILL LAST," A WEDDING POEM
    FOR MICHAEL AND SHONDA

CHAPTER 27
THE GOLDEN CLOUD

October 25, 2020

Dear Rosie, Dass, and Evangeline,

As a boy, I grew up listening to radio songs about love.

These emotional songs had a powerful impact on me. I formed my ideas about love from them. Songs and movies often portray love as an emotion, so I thought if you were in the right place at the right time, love magically happened to you. Love was out there, waiting to surprise you. When it did, people were happy and willing. But when the love feeling left, they were helpless victims.

I wrongly thought romantic love was an elusive mood—here today, gone tomorrow. I thought romantic love was a feeling.

Many people view love this way. This wrong idea of love dominates our culture.

Growing up, I thought pursuing romantic love meant pursuing good feelings at all costs. I thought feelings validated or invalidated love relationships. I thought love would feel like the chorus of a Journey song, when Steve Perry hits the high notes and I get goose bumps on my arms. I didn't know when love would happen, but when it did, I was convinced it would feel amazing. To me, romantic love was an elusive thing, mysterious and dazzling, like a Golden Cloud.

My early experience with love—or what I thought was love—was seeking emotional experiences. I was looking for someone who could make me feel. In junior high and high school, I mistook these initial feelings of attraction as love, so I was constantly pursuing those early relationship highs. Predictably, when the feelings of newness wore off, I moved on and started looking for that Golden Cloud feeling again.

The Golden Cloud is an emotionally passive view of love. And wherever it leads, there is the gold dust of attraction. There is possibility, romance, and bliss. In the Golden Cloud, there is no negativity, no hardship or work. Only starry-night kisses. Only whimsy and dancing in the rain. To stay in love, we must follow its whims. Love is validated by emotion. The Golden Cloud of love comes and goes at random, and we must follow it.

But when those feelings start to fade, we think something is wrong. We panic! Maybe we are falling out of love? Without overwhelming feelings of desire, maybe it is time to move on? We think our romantic relationships are at the mercy of this whimsical thing, this Golden Cloud, and there is nothing we can do about it.

Most loving relationships have cycles and seasons. And at the beginning they are full of new relationship energy. Everything is charged with emotion. Every text. The first hug. Hand hold. Kiss. The first "I love you." Everything is a rush. It feels intoxicating. Over time, it is normal for this to change, to even out. The emotions don't go away, but they don't feel like a tornado anymore. This often happens several months or a few years into the relationship. If we believe the lies of the Golden Cloud, our lack of emotions create a crisis. For some, this crisis of emotion provides justification to leave.

I'm just not feeling it anymore. My lack of feelings means I must stop any loving act toward you. To stay with you without feelings breaks the laws of the universe. I'm sorry. This is simply beyond my control. I must obey the Golden Cloud.

The Golden Cloud is a reversal of things. Love is no longer a decisive and willful action toward another person, an object, or God. Love itself becomes the object. Its whims are more important than people, commitments, and even God.

When love becomes our god, we lose our faith when feelings go away.

When love becomes our god, we demand that our lover give us strong feelings.

When love becomes our god, our focus is not on the other but on our experience.

The Golden Cloud demands bliss but gives little or nothing in return. When love becomes our god, we aren't looking for a relationship with a person but a fix. We aren't looking to know someone or be loving to someone; we are looking for a rush.

Pulitzer Prize–winning author Ernest Becker called this "apocalyptic romance." He wrote, "The love partner becomes the divine ideal within which to fulfill one's life... We want redemption—nothing less."

When love becomes our god, we look to it for ultimate meaning. We think love will make us whole. *Love will heal me. Love will fill the places, insecurities, and hurts inside me.* But no earthly love can fill our deepest places. No love will stand up under the impossible weight of those expectations. Love will not fill your appetite. A significant other cannot complete you. Lovers, husbands and wives, even the great ones, are poor substitutes for God.

God is love, but love is not and will never be God.

Maybe the fastest way for us to know love is by giving it away. Jesus was right when he said, "It is more blessed to give than to receive." As long as we make people into objects of our desire and demand feelings and fulfillment from them, we position ourselves for a lifetime of misery. George MacDonald, the mentor of C. S. Lewis, wrote, "The one principle of hell is—'I am my own. I am my own king and my own subject. *I* am the centre from which go out my thoughts; *I* am the object and end of my thoughts; back upon *me* as the alpha and omega of life, my thoughts return. My own glory is, and ought to be, my chief care; my ambition, to gather the regards of men to the one centre, myself. My pleasure is *my* pleasure.'"

Love pursues. Love first pursued us. Loving another is not an emotion we follow but a person we pursue. Believing the lies of the Golden Cloud makes us believe we are passive, helpless victims. Love is not something that happens to us; it is something we create with care, time, and intention. Romantic love is something you and your person build together. Love is a way of being. And love is knowing each other, which always deepens with time.

I love you,
Dad

CHAPTER 28
PURSUIT AND PEACE

October 31, 2020

Dear Rosie, Dass, and Evangeline,

Tonight, Rosie, you dressed up as a hunter. I loved your braided hair and hunting cloak. You carried my red bow, the same bow I had when I was your age. Dass, you dressed up as an officer, and your blue uniform matched your pretty eyes. You had a badge and fingerless gloves. Evangeline, you wore a shiny blue Elsa dress and looked radiant. I started the night as a baseball player but became a horse, and you sat on my shoulders as we went from house to house. Ms. Daniella came with us, and she was a lovely cowgirl.

In the last letter, we talked about romantic love as an action word. It is a heart longing and a pursuit of a person. It is an intention, a move in a direction. In his poem "The Song of Wandering Aengus," William Butler Yeats wrote,

> I will find out where she has gone,
> And kiss her lips and take her hands;
> And walk among long dappled grass,

151

And pluck till time and times are done,

The silver apples of the moon,

The golden apples of the sun.

Romance is an active pursuit. It is not passive like the Golden Cloud. Romance is taking up the chase; it is pursuing and finding the one your heart loves. Romance has an infinite quality to it; inspiring generations of songwriters, screenwriters, and poets. Every poem is right, and every song is true. They are all true. Romance is the language of the stolen heart.

In romance, there is a pursuer, and there is one being pursued.

Most boys are not great at pursuing. Some men are not either. Some are passive; they like you but don't pursue you. They wait for you to initiate. Others are too direct, or too needy, or too impatient. Others are consumed with trying to impress you. You can learn a lot about a man's character by how he pursues you.

Many high school girls want the cute guy to show them attention. The one who is tall and handsome, maybe even good at sports. The girls work, plot, and do anything they can to get him to respond. They fawn all over him, blinking their eyes and playing with their hair and laughing too loud around him. They smile and stare and obsess over him and treat him like they are fans of his boy band.

There is nothing wrong with dressing up, smiling, and saying hello back to a guy who says hello to you. But you cannot choose or control who pursues you. You can only control yourselves. Don't be like those fangirls who feel desperate. You can't love someone you don't respect. Not romantically, anyway. So don't fawn and flirt and try to control the situation. Don't beg for attention or advertise yourselves like many girls do.

Some girls (and boys too) are addicted to attention seeking. I talked about this in a previous letter, how social media can promote this. Some girls and boys constantly post pictures of themselves online in hopes of getting that rush of attention. They want that next like, heart, comment. These pictures feel like advertising. Lonely and desperate. *Do you see me? Do you approve?*

Lonely people used to go to bars to seek attention. They would sit at the bar, dress flashy, and make themselves available to anyone who might come along. People used to advertise in bars; now they advertise on social media. Social media is the new virtual bar.

Desperate and lonely groping leads to a desperate and lonely heart. You will find peace when you move away from attention seeking and affection grasping. Guard your hearts. Be careful what and who you allow into them. Be mindful of the conversations you have, the things you see with your eyes and listen to with your ears. Be careful of asking people for validation, giving them power over you. Your hearts are precious, and it is your life. So be pretty, gorgeous, captivating. But don't scramble for a man to notice you. The right man will value you just as you are. As a character in the movie *The Secret Life of Walter Mitty* observed, "Beautiful things don't ask for attention."

When you don't try to control the situation, you find peace. Be okay whether the cute guy notices you or not. Sure, it feels good if he does. But be happy, content, and fulfilled if he does not smile back at you or ask you to the prom.

These rejections happen to everyone. They can be crushing. If you feel rejected, please remember, you have so much to offer. You do. And it's not your job to convince the cute guy or anyone else of that. It hurts when you like a boy and he doesn't like you back. Respect yourself enough to let him go, and wait for one who cherishes you.

Some men will use the words "I love you" or "I'm sorry" to try to manipulate you. They may do something awful and then say, "But

I love you, honey." Nope. No, he doesn't, or he would not have done that. Believe patterns, not words.

Watch how the guy you like treats his mom. Is he kind to her and to you? Watch how his parents interact, because they are his "normal," and their behavior may be what he expects from you. Is he faithful and loyal? Examine his friends carefully. They say a lot about him. Does he listen to you? Does he respect you and value you? Does he think you are the best thing that has ever happened to him, or do you feel overlooked? Don't ignore the red flags, those warning signs that something isn't quite right. The red flags you ignore in the beginning often come back to hurt you later.

Can he keep a job? Can he provide for you? Do you feel protected by him, both physically and emotionally? Or do you feel unsafe? Stay far, far away from a man who makes you feel unsafe. Does he lead you spiritually? What do your friends think about him? What do your parents think? If your friends or parents have reservations, pause. There is no need to rush. If someone is the one, he will still be the one in a year too.

If you are thinking about getting married, go to counseling together. Watch how honest he is there. Can he take constructive criticism? It takes a humble and open man to do this. What was he like in his past relationships? Watch how he handles conflict. Is he patient? Or does he erupt? Does he blame you for everything? Or does he share his heart with kindness, even when he is frustrated? Is he wise with money? Or is he impulsive, always going into debt?

Challenge him, but do it in a humble and respectful way. A strong man will be fine, even impressed by this. But an insecure man won't let you challenge him and won't ever accept you "winning." He has to have the last word. He will mansplain and talk over you. Don't marry a man like this. You will feel devalued and alone.

Keep yourselves sexually pure. Your hearts and bodies belong to you and to God, not to any man. Some men may feel entitled to your bodies, but they can keep their groping and grubby hands off you. If a man cannot wait for you, he may not have self-control after he has you. Make him prove himself by having self-control before you get married. Your bodies are gifts to give your future husbands. Wait for him.

If you think a man is a project and you need to fix him, he is not the one for you. Don't spend your life trying to control and coerce someone to change. Both of you will end up frustrated, and he will feel rejected and disrespected. And most people don't change. If you think marrying someone will change him or change you, it will not. How your relationship feels before you say "I do" is how it will feel the day after you say it.

Be patient. Don't choose someone out of loneliness. We often make our worst choices when we are lonely. It's better to be single and sometimes lonely than with someone and wish you were single.

The best relationships are with friends who are loyal, committed, and believe in the best for you. The best friends know your full story and still love and accept you. They share your values and beliefs. These are the best ones eventually, over time, to love as more than friends. Keep your eyes open for a man with your same values, which are the values in this book. Someone who knows the Father, who is kind, thankful, brave, and humble. A man who works hard and can protect you and provide for you.

If a man does pursue you, open your heart a little at a time. Don't gush. Keep your secrets. Don't tell him your life story or hold out your heart too soon. Don't place all your hopes in him. He's just a man. Be patient. Love will grow and blossom when it is time. The right man will be patient and pursue you, and you will learn his heart and character and know if he is the right one. Don't date someone who is not right for you. Don't date someone you know you won't marry. Don't waste your time or string him along.

You are rare and beautiful treasures.

You can have full, rich lives if you remain single. Many people feel pressured to get married by this or that age, and I hope you never feel that way. Some of the best days of my life were when I was single and close to my spiritual family and friends, with Jon and others. There are many single women and men in the world who never get married. Or maybe they get married and a spouse passes away.

My grandmother Helen was single for twenty-nine years after her husband passed. She never remarried but was full of joy. She had many friends and a strong spiritual family who loved her. She raised us with Nana. She was present for us and loved us, and we loved her. She had a best friend, Vernon. They had lunch together every day. Every Thanksgiving, Vernon came to our house, and he was like family.

The best place to be is at peace. Protect your peace. Don't be desperate. You can't have peace if you are desperate. You can't have peace if you constantly worry about who likes you or not. Peace is beautiful. So keep your peace and trust God's good plan for you, whether that involves a man or not.

Trusting God will give you peace "which transcends all understanding." Here's the full verse from Philippians: "Do not be anxious about anything, but in every situation, by prayer and petition, with thanksgiving, present your requests to God. And the peace of God, which transcends all understanding, will guard your hearts and your minds in Christ Jesus." When you are anxious, take a deep breath and pray and remember this verse. The peace comes *after* prayer and thanksgiving.

> Be patient and protect your peace,
> Dad

PART 8

DREAMS
AND LEGACY

CHAPTER 29

DREAMS

November 5, 2020

Dear Rosie, Dass, and Evangeline,

I never reached my dream to play for the Red Sox. My chances to make the pros were always slim. The computer says 0.0296 percent of Little League baseball players make the majors. Nana never told me about the odds. She never discouraged me, tried to edit my dreams, or pushed her dreams on me. She just cheered for me as I chased mine. We played catch in the backyard. The same backyard where you girls played hide-and-seek. She took me to watch the Red Sox.

I tried. I worked hard. I lifted weights. I hit thousands and thousands of baseballs. I learned practice makes permanent, and if I repeated good habits, they would translate to the game. In the ninth grade, I knew my high school needed a baseball team. I talked to the high school coaches once a week until they finally said yes. The next two years we started a baseball team and played in the state championships. Then I played baseball in college. Pursuing a dream is exciting, but it is also a grind. You have to fight for your dreams.

I remember watching a Red Sox game when I was about four-teen. We were talking to a family sitting next to us. The dad asked what I was going to do when I grew up. I never told people my dream. I didn't want people to laugh or tell me I was foolish. But something bold came over me. I pointed to the field and said, "I'm gonna play baseball for them." But instead of laughing, the man said, "I will watch for you." This is rare. Many people won't accept your big dreams. They will just laugh and say, "Good luck with that" or "You need a backup plan."

But don't worry about the cynics or the scoffers. This is your life. So dream big. Time will tell if your dreams will happen; it's not for them to decide.

Your great-grandfather George was an engineer and gifted with his hands and building things. He built some of the furniture in my cabin. His mother, Nettie, who is your great-great-grandmother, was a tremendous artist and painter, painting dishes and cups and wild-life. Uncle Bill is a bike racer; he can ride over one hundred miles on his bike in a day. My great-uncle Alvin played Major League Baseball.

Your family is full of creative and gifted dreamers. Just like you.

Every dreamer started somewhere and failed many times along the way. Don't be so afraid to fail that you don't try. Comfort is often the death of dreams. So is fear. As long as your dreams stay locked away in your minds, it stays safe but unknown. No one will criticize you or call you crazy. Your dreams are safe when they are secret, but they will never grow wings and fly unless you take that first bold step. How many dreams and ideas are locked away inside minds and never revealed to the world? How many great books go unwritten, songs unsung, and movements unborn?

Don't let fear keep you from taking that first bold step. Actor Jim Carrey said,

Fear is going to be a player in your life, but you get to decide how much. You can spend your whole life imagining ghosts, worrying about the pathway to the future. But all there will ever be is what's happening here and the decisions we make in this moment, which are based in either love or fear. So many of us choose our path out of fear disguised as practicality. What we really want seems impossibly out of reach and ridiculous to expect. So we never dare to ask the universe for it. . . .

My father could have been a great comedian, but he didn't believe that that was possible for him. And so he made a conservative choice. Instead, he got a safe job as an accountant, and when I was twelve years old, he was let go from that safe job, and our family had to do whatever we could to survive. I learned many great lessons from my father, not the least of which was that you can fail at what you don't want, so you might as well take a chance on doing what you love.

You girls have dreams too. We talk about them sometimes. A dream is active and moving; it is something we participate in, something we shape. Always remember that a dream without work is just a wish.

If you don't have to work hard for it, your dream is too small. Dreaming the big dream is the easy part. But many people don't want to put in the hours, months, and years to achieve their dreams. Others burn out when they lose sight of the dream. Visualize your dreams and keep them right in front of you; they will inspire you to do the work. If you only look at the work, it can be daunting and overwhelming.

As you grow, you will learn more about yourselves and how you were created. You will discover your gifts and find things that ignite your hearts. You will have dreams, and sometimes your dreams will change. A boy named Joseph dreamed his brothers would bow down to him, then years later they did. But when he was young, Joseph did not see how big the dream really was. His dream was just about him and his brothers and how they would bow down to him.

As you grow, your dreams grow too. As you learn love and compassion and empathy, your dreams will become much bigger than you first imagined.

My dream grew too. I played baseball and loved it. Looking back, my pursuit of baseball was more about chasing fame and validation. For me, baseball was a means to an end. It could have been football or basketball or karate or anything really. I wanted to find acceptance and fame through performance. I thought if I was successful enough, one day I would be famous and find applause and validation from others.

But in college, I began to see that people's applause would not fulfill me the way I thought it would. I was playing baseball but grew disillusioned and frustrated. And it was a good frustration because it made me ask questions. And my dream began to change.

Joseph, too, had chances to quit along the way. He had many chances to make the wrong decision or to keep quiet. But he kept believing, even though the path to his dream was jagged and uneven. Joseph went through struggles, opposition, criticisms, and false accusations. He could have easily quit or stopped believing it would happen. But he did not. And the dream unfolded as he kept walking.

After many struggles and hardships, Joseph's dream was fulfilled. His dream began as a vision of fame. But over time, as he grew and the Lord was with him, his dream evolved and changed and saved many lives.

I hope your dreams keep growing too. I hope they are so big that unless God helps you, they are doomed to fail. I hope you have the courage to pursue what you love. When hardships come, keep walking. Every dream begins with a step.

Dream big dreams,
Dad

CHAPTER 30

DEDICATION

November 10, 2020

Dear Rosie, Dass, and Evangeline,

Recently, I was in Barnes and Noble doing a book signing. A young boy, about eight, approached the table, nudged forward by his father. The boy stared at me, determined. After a few moments, he asked, "How do I become a writer?"

"Well," I said, "do you like using a pen, pencil, computer, or typewriter?"

"Computer," he said.

"Good. Me too," I replied. "If you can write, if you can put down words, you are a writer now. You don't need a book deal or a publisher or anyone to give you permission. Fall in love with language, poems, and songs that move your heart. Fall in love with great stories, the ones you cannot put down. The main thing every writer needs to know is this: you are a writer *now*."

The boy smiled and shook my hand.

We often look to others for validation. *Do you accept my dream?* I think this is true of most of us, me included, at times. We often believe our dreams will come to us someday in the distant future. One old day, when we have gray hair growing out of our ears, King Aragorn will appear at our door and ask us to kneel. Then he will tap our shoulders with his sword and say, "Arise."

We believe that one day we will finally arrive.

Don't wait for one day. Begin now.

For many, dreams are a destination filled with applause at the end or nothing at all. But as long as we strain to be popular, we may lose ourselves. Or take shortcuts, trying to be like someone else. Our voices become an echo of an original. But echoes have diminishing returns. They become weaker with each reverberation.

Don't wait for others to validate your dreams before you take the first step.

Work from your silent, inner mandate and divine impulses. Listen to the small voice that says, "I must." Work from a divine mandate, and you won't worry as much about pleasing others. You may create things that never make you famous or popular. You may never go viral. You may get criticized. Begin anyway.

Pursuing your dreams requires dedication, and dedication requires us to begin and begin again. Dedication is one of the best lessons you can learn. Right now, you girls go to school and church; you play soccer, basketball, and tennis. Sometimes you do gymnastics, and you swim. Even more than the sports, what I hope you learn is dedication. The best girls on your soccer team, like V, never miss a soccer practice. They practice at home, go to soccer camps, and sometimes take private lessons. They watch YouTube videos of soccer players, work out and run, and play on multiple teams. And when they stop playing soccer someday, whether that is after high school, college, or a professional career, they will have learned the value of dedication.

Whatever your dreams are, I hope you dedicate yourself.

When Ed was a boy, he saw two older kids playing guitar and was mesmerized. Right then, he knew he wanted to play. He daydreamed, flipping through an old Sears catalog, looking at pictures of electric guitars, and earmarking the pages. But he realized he couldn't buy one. So he stopped looking.

When I asked Ed about it, this is what he said:

I dreamed about playing guitar. I knew it was what I wanted to do. But when I realized I had no money and couldn't buy one and there was nobody in our small town to teach me, I quit looking. But mom didn't forget. She didn't dismiss it. She remembered. She was determined to find better opportunities for me.

When she got a new job, we moved away from our trailer into a Houston suburb. Not long after, mom surprised me with a five-dollar acoustic guitar from a yard sale. It was old. It played horribly. The strings were so high. It was so hard to make a chord or play a single note. It was perfect.

Months later, mom found a guitar teacher in a small music store in a strip mall. When I stepped out of my first lesson, I remember seeing a shining red guitar hanging on the wall. And Mom encouraged me to play it. She had not forgotten my earmarked Sears guitars. She was going to make sure I had a real guitar. Now she had a better job and could buy one for me. So she bought it. To this day, I've never felt more excited about a guitar. That night I couldn't sleep. I just lay there—staring at that guitar for hours.

The next day, I got huge blisters on my fingers learning how to play "No Sleep Till Brooklyn." It was the first song I learned on my own—playing by ear. I was so proud of those blisters. I listened and played anything, country and rock and rap. The first solo I learned was Led Zeppelin's "Whole Lotta Love." I loved that old red guitar. I played every day for hours and dedicated myself to being the best guitar player possible.

I asked Ed about some of his old bandmates, from his first band when he was sixteen, and what they are doing now. He said he knew many other musicians and guitar players who were far superior to him. He told me how talented some of them were. Some of them were not playing anymore because they made bad choices. Others were lazy or did not dedicate themselves to their dream. There were more talented players, people who stopped playing guitar because they did not do the work to be great. Where would they be now if they had dedicated themselves? Would they be professional musicians too? Maybe? Probably?

I never knew them, but it made me sad. Sad for what might have been. It made me wonder how many people never reach their full potential. How many people start off brilliantly but quit somewhere along the way? How many people never dedicate themselves, or get discouraged and stop just before the breakthrough happens?

Being dedicated to our dreams is also about stewardship. Stewardship means being faithful with what God has given us. It is developing the gifts God gave us and using them for the common good. Like in the parable of the talents, some people dedicate and multiply their talents. Other people are lazy and never develop. They waste their lives. People who are lazy miss out on their destinies and deprive the world of their gifts. Many people never reach their potential because they quit.

Dedication matters. Stewardship matters.

Here's a secret: Most books never get published, and most

bands never get heard. Most dreams are never reached. The ones who succeed are the ones who fall down and get up and keep going. Keep going. Dreams require toughness, hard work, and practice to learn your craft and keep going when you fail or lose, when you get rejected or criticized.

Dreams require fight.

Keep going,
Dad

CHAPTER 31
DEDICATION (TIPS)

November 20, 2020

Dear Rosie, Dass, and Evangeline,

We spoke of dedication as a way to reach your dreams. Remember: a dream without work is just a wish. I want to highlight a few things to keep in mind as you dedicate and work and pursue your dreams. Here are four tips to help you along the way:

1. *Attach yourselves to the hip of a master.*

Find the best teacher at whatever it is you want to learn. With the internet and the many resources available to you, this makes your search much easier. There are also virtual classes and videos, master classes and podcasts, and ways to connect with someone who has mastered whatever it is you want to do.

Millions of young women are confident and smart and talented. But many of them try to make it alone. There is only so much you can achieve alone. Most young people spend years trying to figure out a craft and finally start excelling in their thirties or forties. But if you find and learn from a master of any profession, sport, or activity, you can speed up your own mastery and accelerate your growth. You can excel much sooner, maybe in your teens or twenties.

In addition to baseball, I fell in love with tracking wildlife when I was seven. Nana signed me up for the Big Brothers program so I'd have a consistent, positive male role model in my life. My first mentor was Tom, and he was great. Then I met Sonny, who loved the outdoors. Sonny was a great mentor to me. He had a dog, a Doberman named Gus. He had huge paws and was fast. I remember running through piles of fall leaves, Gus crashing along right behind me.

Sonny started taking me deer hunting. The first thing we did was to look for signs of deer. I learned how to find and identify tracks, rubs, and scrapes. I wasn't old enough to carry a bow or a gun, but Sonny taught me how to walk without making a sound, to avoid old leaves and twigs and things that were loud underfoot. He taught me to be mindful of the wind direction and sun on my face, and how to use shadows. How to slow down and listen and use all my senses. Sometimes, when the wind is blowing, you can smell animals before you see them.

Sonny always found deer. Always. One time, we trailed a big buck for two hours, and when we came back to the start of the trail, the buck had circled us and left fresh tracks in my bootprints! I was amazed—and hooked. Tracking engaged my senses and woke something in me. Ever since, I've loved using my senses to find and follow wild animals. You girls see deer at our cabin. And we have coyotes, raccoons, and two bobcats. One bobcat walked right up to our porch.

Sonny is a master tracker. Walking through the woods beside him, I learned his rhythms and patterns and how to track and hunt. I spent hundreds of hours with him in the woods, and by the time I was a teenager, I was a good tracker.

Whatever you want to do, find a master and learn from him or her.

I've had many other great teachers and mentors. Keith is my karate instructor, and he's one of the best in the world. He competes at international levels. I wanted to learn how to grapple, so I went to California to spend some time with the Gracie family, the best of the best in martial arts. I had some great coaches in high school, including Coach Smith, Coach Norwood, and Coach Russell, and a baseball genius, R. C. I had great writing teachers—Mrs. Holeman, Mrs. Cordon, and Dr. Downs and Dr. Root in college,—and many others. I read great books on writing, listen to podcasts, and watch videos from people who are masters. I've had many mentors, coaches, and people who poured into my life. I hope you have the same.

Be teachable. Listen. If you are not teachable, you put limits on yourselves. The best at any profession, sport, or activity all have great coaches. Every Olympian, athlete, writer, business leader, and president has coaches, teachers, or mentors. Every one. Having a mentor requires you to be humble and teachable and to listen.

You are responsible for whomever you choose as a teacher. When you are young, your parents pick your coaches. When you are older, you decide. So watch. Listen. Learn who is the best. Do not attach yourselves to someone who is lazy, has bad character, or is overly negative. Watch closely before committing your life and precious time to them.

2. Find a few people who believe in you.

I remember a time in my life when writing was hard and prospects for publishing my book looked bleak. For the most part, I have persisted and believed I'm supposed to write. But I remember this one season when I was discouraged and tired. It didn't look like writing was going to work out. I told my friend Jessie I was thinking about quitting. She said, "No. You are a good writer, and people need that book. What you are doing is important." I don't think she realized it, but that conversation was a tipping point for me. It kept me from quitting and gave me the courage to persist.

The old African proverb is true: "If you want to go fast, go alone. If you want to go far, go together."

I'm blessed to have many friends who believe in me. I have a few close friends I share my ideas with. I bounce things off of them and get their feedback, and they usually have a different perspective or something valuable to add. Or a positive nudge in the right direction.

The people you allow to speak into your lives are a sacred choice.

Some people submit to the wrong person or friend circle. Don't join a friend circle just because it is full of the popular kids. Don't blindly follow people because they are the loudest voices in the room or most sure of themselves or most persuasive.

Find friends who are not overly critical of you. Critical people, especially friends, can influence you negatively. They can slow down your dreams. Remember the words of Teddy Roosevelt: "It is not the critic who counts." Friends should challenge you, but they should not be overly critical of you. There is a difference.

One thing I loved about being in Portland was that many people there identified themselves by their dreams. They might have said something like "I am a writer," but in their day-to-day lives they were restaurant waiters. But they already believed who they were and where they wanted to be. It takes courage to step into your dreams this way. And if you have a few close friends who believe in you, you can do anything.

3. Don't feed the trolls.

Part of finding your voice is allowing others to challenge and speak direction into your lives. King Solomon once said, "A wise man is impressed by a rebuke." Be open to criticism, especially from friends you trust. But don't listen to the trolls.

Social media is full of trolls. Critics and name-callers and online bullies. People say critical things online for the same reason school bullies do: trying to feel better about themselves by putting others down. It's drama, one-upmanship, and attention grabbing. Trolls are an unpleasant and ill-smelling sort. Do not respond to them or let them lure you into their drama. Don't even read their words in the first place. Stay far away from their dark and moldy caves.

The more you put yourselves out into the world, the more trolls will come at you. I've had my share of them. But don't respond to your critics. It's not worth your time or energy. Just let them sneer and snicker and be warty and troll-like. You focus on your dreams and go about being secretly awesome.

The critics who matter are the ones you know and respect. They want the best for you. A good coach or mentor who knows you and wants the best for you is usually the right place to start. Ask, "Does this person love me and want the best for me?" "Is this person seeking my good?" "Or is this about trolling or shaming or something else?"

4. *Practice while others sleep.*

When it comes to your dreams, practice matters. Practice does not make perfect; it makes permanent. Learn to do it the right way, and then practice until it becomes an ingrained habit. To pursue your dreams and master your craft, you will need to practice hard and practice at home.

Practicing a few hours a week will not be enough for mastery. Dedicate yourselves in ways that others do not. It means saying no when others say yes. When others go out to parties and stay up late and do all sorts of other things, let them. You go to work. Stay focused. Go to the gym or the workshop or the laboratory of your dreams.

Some people fail on purpose. It's like a preemptive strike on fear. It's another type of quitting. They think, *If I don't get to the finish line, I don't have to face my fear.* They quit before trying. Abolitionist leader Henry Ward Beecher said,

> Hold yourself responsible for a higher standard than anybody else expects of you. . . . Never excuse yourself to yourself. Never pity yourself. Be a hard master to yourself, but lenient to everybody else.

Surround yourselves with people who are better than you. Whenever you are trying to accomplish anything great, train with people who are more experienced, more capable, more accomplished than you are. Don't avoid a challenge. Challenge yourselves, and it will make you better. And when you can, work and practice with people who have already accomplished the goals you are trying to reach.

The people who make it are often not the most talented ones. They are the ones who have learned how to dedicate and never give up. Someone once said, "Hard work beats talent when talent doesn't work hard."

Don't be one of those people who never find out who they are or what they can achieve. Dream big dreams, dedicate, and work hard to reach them. Always remember your vision and your heart.

I believe in you,
Dad

CHAPTER 32
RESISTANCE

November 25, 2020

Dear Rosie, Dass, and Evangeline,

I recently spoke to the Other Rosie and asked her what kind of dedication it took for her to go from a young girl who liked swimming to an Olympian. I wanted to know how she got started, how she trained, and how she eventually made Team Canada. She said,

> When I was young, I switched from swimming to water polo because I had a crush on a boy. I did water polo because I wanted him to notice me, I wanted to impress him. I went to practice because he was there. But through the years, I developed the heart and vision to be an Olympian. It was my vision that pulled me through the hard moments and the resistance when it felt impossible and I wanted to quit.
>
> I remember one time, I did want to quit. It was a hard year; I wasn't doing well. I remember not wanting to go to practice. But I got up anyway and dragged myself to the pool at 7:00 a.m. About an hour later, I was having a blast and laughing with my

teammates. I learned a lesson that day. I learned that my attitude, my mindset was a huge key for me to accomplish my vision. My mindset and emotions can fluctuate, they can shift quickly. I can feel terrible, but if I stay committed to my vision, I get out of the dark cloud. This helped me again and again on my way to making Team Canada. So every time I didn't want to practice or I wanted to quit, I made the choice to show up. I made the decision, every day, to keep my commitment and keep going, no matter how I felt.

I think most people don't realize this is one of the secrets to greatness. Most people don't realize what is available to them if they keep their commitments. The way we access greatness is to keep our small commitments and follow through, over and over again. It seems like a secret. But it's not a secret. If we put in the hard work and dedicate, if we can learn to overcome defeats, especially at a young age, we can have access to greatness for the rest of our lives.

As you pursue your dreams, you will face resistance. Sometimes resistance comes from the outside. Unfair coaches and referees. Teachers who, for some reason, don't like you or give you the wrong grade. Classmates or teammates who try to sabotage you or steal your ideas. Maybe injuries like a sprained ankle or broken wrist.

Resistance comes in many forms. Some resistance comes from inside, from within you and your mindset. This resistance is sneaky and harder to detect. It may be harder to overcome than external resistance. It is the thing that says, *Don't get out of bed*, and makes you want to hit the snooze button instead of waking up and getting to work. It discourages you and makes your dream look like an impossible mountain. It is lurking around and often comes at you after a failure, making you want to quit. *See? I knew you would never make it.*

Resistance pushes us to keep things as they currently are. *Stay at home. Stay comfortable. Don't take any bold steps. Don't take risks.* Resistance wanted to keep Bilbo in the Shire. Resistance wanted to keep Luke on Tatooine. Resistance will stop us by any means necessary. Distraction. Fear. Anxiety. It will use any excuse, real or imagined, to stop our pursuit of the dream. Resistance wants to keep us living in what Henry David Thoreau called "quiet desperation."

Your emotions will go up and down. They will change and move and challenge you to quit. One day you will feel like you can conquer the world. The next day you might not want to get out of bed. Keep going, keep your vision, keep showing up. Your emotions don't have final say over your decisions.

Resistance is cunning. It snakes up to us after a defeat, loss, or failure and hisses in our ears, telling us to quit. It wants us to accept defeat. Defeats can crush us, or they can teach us resilience.

History is filled with examples of great leaders who rose after defeats. Michael Jordan was cut from his high school basketball team to later become one of the best basketball players of all time. He said, "Everybody goes through disappointments. It's how you overcome those disappointments. . . . I just wasn't good enough. . . . The best thing that happened to me was to get cut because it made me go back and get caught up with my skill level."

Abraham Lincoln failed in politics many times before he was finally elected president. Remember, there was something greater going on. God was at work behind the scenes. If Lincoln had been elected president sooner, he would not have led our nation during the Civil War. He would not have signed the Emancipation Proclamation. Who knows how history would have turned out? God was working in Lincoln's failures. Lincoln was elected "for such a time as this."

I remember when I was in college, my senior year of baseball. By then, I already knew the Red Sox dream was not going to happen. Halfway through the season, I had a great game, got three hits . . . but didn't play again. I didn't really play again for the remaining twenty games.

It didn't make sense. It was my senior year, I had worked hard for four years, I never missed practice or a workout, and statistically, I was the second-best hitter on the team. I felt like I had earned the right to play. We had a great assistant coach who later became the head coach, and he agreed with me, I should be playing. It was confusing and also felt like the death of my long-held dream. I knew before my senior year that I wasn't going to play baseball professionally. It was frustrating to not get a chance.

After the season, my heart let go of that dream. I returned to writing. I returned to books and stories and all the things I loved since I was a boy visiting the library with my grandmother. I started writing fiction. I read The Lord of the Rings. But my senior year of college, in the middle of my frustration, I had no idea I would become a writer. After I let go of baseball, writing seemed to surface in my heart and happen naturally.

Sometimes when one door closes, another one opens.

I loved writing, but publishing a book proved difficult.

After college and several years of earnest writing, someone encouraged me to get an agent. An agent has relationships with publishers and can open doors. Most of the major publishing houses do not even accept unsolicited manuscripts—meaning, unless you have an agent, they won't even read your proposal and your chapters. So I tried to get an agent.

I think when you feel called to do something, you are emboldened. When you believe a task is connected with your purpose, with the reason God put you on the earth, you find courage. Writing felt like that to me. It still does.

When I pursued an agent, it felt deep and necessary. I had things to say, things I was supposed to say and write. So I assumed it would work out, and this was the next step. Get an agent. Become a writer. I thought I needed an agent to keep pursing my dream and doing the thing I felt called to do.

I worked for months, writing my best chapters, drafting a proposal, and sending letters to agents. I didn't hear back from any of them. I kept trying. Months became years. I contacted over fifty agents. I heard back from only three. Two were rude. One wrote me, "This is weak," and nothing else. Another one was constructive, saying, "This is a good message and your writing has potential." He didn't like it enough to say yes, but gave me honest feedback. I was grateful for that. I took his constructive criticism and rewrote everything one more time. Then I sent it back to him, but he didn't respond.

After several years of trying to get an agent, I knew it was not going to happen. I had struck out. But something inside me wouldn't let me quit. Some inner mandate called me to keep going, to keep writing.

Also, something changed within me. I decided to write because I had something to say. For me, being an author is not about being famous or published or anything like that. It is not about being known but being heard. I decided I would only put words out into the world that I felt were necessary and needed. I decided if no one wanted them, I would self-publish in blogs or books or wherever I could. If words burned inside of me, then I would write them and put them into the world. I stopped asking for permission.

Even though I did not have an agent, I decided to try once more to get published. It was five years after those initial letters to agents were rejected. I decided to try without an agent. I sent out random emails with my proposal and chapters to several publishers. I didn't have email addresses. I didn't know one person at any of the publishing houses. I sent several messages to info@ or contact@ emails. I guessed at what I thought were email addresses, taking shots in the dark.

I kept writing my book, whether I got a book deal or not. Six months after I sent those emails, I was close to finishing and intended to self-publish. But then I finally got an email back. It was from my favorite publisher, HarperCollins. They loved my writing. They believed in the message and offered me a deal. They apologized for taking so long to get back with me, saying there were several thousand emails in that inbox. Somehow, they opened my email, read it, and loved it. I didn't need an agent after all.

As you pursue your dreams, you will encounter resistance. Sometimes it will feel unfair. It is the shade, the shadow side of your dream. Remember to keep showing up, like the Other Rosie did, no matter how she felt. Keep your little commitments and do them faithfully, even when no one is watching. Keep working on your craft, even if people call you weak. When you do, you will learn one secret to greatness.

Greatness is available to you.

It lives on the other side of resistance.

I believe in you,
Dad

CHAPTER 33

TIME

December 24, 2020

Dear Rosie, Dass, and Evangeline,

When I was your age, time felt like an endless resource.

Time felt as if it would never run out for me, my friends, or my family. It was captured in feelings and moments and memories. My first hit playing for the Coyotes. My first bike ride without training wheels on my black-and-gray Huffy. Nana running along beside me, helping me balance. I rode that bike around the block, standing up as I pedaled, feeling the wind on my face, going as fast as I could.

Time felt like that. Free and windy and infinite.

Maybe it was always supposed to be this way. Maybe we were created to feel this wild and young and limitless. Like I did as a boy. Maybe time was never intended to run out. Maybe time was only supposed to begin. To start, and never stop. Maybe friends were never supposed to move away. Maybe family members were never supposed to stop breathing and go to an eternal place without us. Maybe we were supposed to be here together all along.

All the natural moments of your lives are measured in seconds, minutes, hours, days, weeks, months, and years. But the supernatural moments of your lives, these things sometimes happen outside of time. There are moments in our lives, glimpses and flashes, when we touch eternity. We know that the angels shout when a lost son or daughter limps back home, back to the Father's house. This victorious limp is an eternal moment. We know there will be singing in heaven around the throne, and I believe sometimes, when we reach up and sing here on earth, by grace, we join that eternal Song.

My grandmother Helen prayed for me. We prayed together at her old church. They had these red velvet cushions up front, where we knelt and took Communion. I remember kneeling beside her. She prayed for me my whole life. And I believe prayers touch eternity, going outside of space and time. Sometimes, I think I can still feel hers.

As I grew older, I started to understand that time is not infinite. It is mortal and passing. My best friend Stephen moved away. My green parakeet, Fred, went to heaven. My grandmother did too. Going to college was exciting, but also a goodbye to friends, teachers, and coaches, to my high school identity and those things I worked so hard to achieve. Even my dreams changed. Over time, they, like all things, became memories. School was now over, and life moved on to the next season.

When I was young, time felt like it was something happening to me. My rhythm was to wake up, then eat oatmeal in front of the television while watching *The Lone Ranger*. Nana took me to school; grandmother brought me home; I'd play outside until dark, eat dinner, read, and go to bed. On Sundays, church. In summer, baseball and the pool. Most of my decisions were made for me. But as I got older, I had more choices. As you get older, you will have more choices too.

When I moved away to college, I realized my choices were my own. No one was there to remind me to make my bed or eat oatmeal or brush my teeth. No one was there to wash my clothes or fix my meals. No one made me go to class! I could have skipped my classes and failed out of college. I could have wasted my time. But I went to my classes and baseball practice and church, and sang on Thursday nights with Jon, Zac, and Stacy. I went to bed at a reasonable hour and even brushed my teeth.

In college, I learned to be intentional. I chose how to spend my life. Someone once said, "We don't spend time; we spend our lives," and I think that's true. How you spend your life is up to you. You can go through life flippantly, wasting, reacting, and letting it happen to you. Or you can focus, living with intention and purpose.

Moses prayed in Psalm 90:12, "Teach us to number our days, that we may gain a heart of wisdom." One way we number our days is by knowing they are limited. Our mortal lives are like vapor, and, one day, they will evaporate. Keep this in the front of your minds; it will help you live with purpose and urgency. It will help you say no to trivial things and time wasters. No to relationships or commitments you don't need.

Remember, every time you say yes to something or someone or to some request, you say no to something or someone else. If you are not careful, your yeses will add up, filling your lives with commitments. Don't say yes to something without considering what it will require of you. You girls are talented, and will be asked by many people to do many things. Be careful what you accept.

Most young people prioritize play, even over responsibilities. Play is good and necessary, but it should not have priority over all your responsibilities. I'm thinking of twenty- and thirtysomethings who still play video games all day and night. Nothing against video games; I've played and like some of them. But when we choose and prioritize play over everything else, over our purpose, we miss our destiny.

As you get older, the finite nature of life comes into focus. As Bob Goff said, "Love God, love people, and do stuff." I agree. Live for God; love your family and close friends. Don't submit to the pressures and whims of others. Have the courage to honor your dreams. Take risks and fail at doing what you love. When you fail, learn. Then get up and keep going.

Don't work too hard. Don't spend so much time chasing your ambitions that you neglect the people who love you, the people you love.

Don't fill your lives with too many things. Don't chase the next and best fashion, dress, car, purse, house. You only need a few things. Make them good things. Chuck Palahniuk wisely said, "The things you used to own, now they own you." Live simple lives. Create space for your souls to breathe. Rest on Sundays. Be thankful and content and free.

Forgive others. Someone once said, "Resentment is like drinking poison and expecting the other person to die." Bitterness poisons you. Don't waste your time rehearsing the bad things that have happened to you. Instead, forgive. Forgiveness sets you free. It is the best way to get past the hurt, to stop letting it affect you. Ask God for the grace to let it go.

Life is precious and fleeting. Remember, you are beautiful and only here for a short time. God has blessed you, so rise up. Spend your lives wisely. Don't just react; be intentional. Make wise choices and find a few good friends. Find out what you love, your calling and heart song. Speak it, live it, and sing it. And one day,

TIME

When you are old and grey and full of sleep,
And nodding by the fire, take down this book,
And slowly read, and dream of the soft look
Your eyes had once, and of their shadows deep;
How many loved your moments of glad grace,
And loved your beauty with love false or true,
But one man [me] loved the pilgrim soul in you.

All my love forever,
Dad

PERSONAL LETTERS
TO MY DAUGHTERS

Rosie,

You are a strong and beautiful leader.

Your name is Sahara Rose, and you are beautiful, even when surrounded by desert. You are strong and naturally take charge in our family, with friends, and in different situations. You are a leader at school and on the soccer field. You give good direction, step into situations, and lead with confidence. You have an unusual leadership gift. I honestly believe you could be president of the United States someday. You don't have to be, but you would be a great one.

You have deep compassion. When Nana passed, I told you girls, "I have good news and hard news." When I told you the hard news, you gave me the sweetest hug and said, "I'm sorry, Daddy."

I said, "Why are you sorry, Rosie?"

You said, "Because Nana was your mom, and you lost your mom." I couldn't believe it. You were just seven years old, but your first response to losing your grandmother was concern for me. Even at seven, you already had the empathy and compassion to understand that I'd lost my mom. I said, "It's okay for you to be sad too." Then we all hugged.

Leadership is a powerful combination of influence, confidence, and intelligence. Leadership is also neutral. It may be used for good or evil. Some leaders inspire people to do good things, while others use leadership to control people. They use fear for terrible things, like invading countries or exploiting the vulnerable. Bring your goodness, compassion, and empathy into leadership. Be a kind leader.

Some of the best leaders in the world, as I write this letter today, are women. Jacinda Ardern is the prime minister of New Zealand, and I thought she did a great job during the pandemic. My friend Korie was on a television show and now spends time helping needy and hungry children in other countries. My friend Lindsey was a business leader and now leads at a place called Onsite, helping people heal.

It is easy for leaders to want to control people. Some leaders micro-manage and get frustrated or angry when people do not do what they want. But people, for the most part, don't want to be controlled. The best leaders use their influence to inspire and to encourage. Not to control or coerce or punish when others make mistakes.

Kind leaders influence through love. Cruel leaders influence through fear and control.

Study leadership. Read books on it. Learn how to speak in front of a crowd. Learn how to write, influence, and inspire others. Learn emotional intelligence, not just book smarts and information. Learn how to have empathy, how to enter another's world and feelings. Pause and take your mind off of the task in front of you and see others.

There are a few books on leadership I recommend. I don't agree with every word of them, but they are full of wisdom for leaders: *The Mentor Leader* by Tony Dungy. *Start with Why* by Simon Sinek. *Good to Great* by Jim Collins. *Dare to Lead* by Brené Brown. *The 21 Irrefutable Laws of Leadership* by John Maxwell. *The Leadership Secrets of Billy Graham* by Harold Myra and Marshall Shelley. There are countless others, but these are good ones to start with.

You are also fierce. This year, I watched you play in a soccer game against girls three years older than you and a foot taller. You were playing defender, sweeper; you stood your ground and stopped the advancing players every time they came. No one got past you. No shots allowed on goal. As a second grader, you ran an eight-minute mile at school and beat everyone by a few minutes, including the boys. Last fall, you tried out and made a new soccer team and were the leading scorer. You played soccer in a boys' league and ran and fought as hard as any of them.

You love to run and work hard, fight and compete. You and I are alike in this way. When I was younger, my brother and I competed every day. We played "horse" with a basketball outside at Nana's. Like you and I do sometimes. Uncle Bill and I played football. Raced bikes. Played board games. He was four years older, so he always won. Always. I tried hard and wanted to beat him so bad. But it never happened. I grew up trying to beat him, and it made me competitive, always wanting to win. I competed hard in karate tournaments and different sports.

Maybe you can beat your sister or teammate or opponent, and maybe even be the best player on the team or the fastest runner in your grade. But what if you could be even better? If you are just trying to beat this person or that person, you may never reach your full potential. What if being the best player on your team or even in the whole league is too low of a bar? In college, I learned to stop competing with others and compete with myself. I got better when I stopped worrying about beating my teammates or opponents, set personal goals, and then worked hard to achieve them. Competing with yourself is the best competition.

Set your heart on being the best, the absolute best you can be. Train hard. Play hard. You will need to train on your own sometimes. At home. In the backyard. Sometimes when it's a little cold or raining. Sometimes you won't feel like it. The sky is the limit for you, like your friend the Other Rosie. Greatness is available to you.

It's good to remember that competing and compassion are different postures. When you compete, you are trying to take the basketball or soccer ball, to beat the opponent and win the game. Your posture is grabbing, claiming, and taking. There certainly are things in life we claim and take. This is a good posture to learn. But the posture of compassion is open hands: *What do you need? How can I help you?* Both postures are important, and it takes wisdom to know when to claim and when to give.

A general rule that helps me is this: When you are competing, like in soccer, be aggressive, be as fierce as possible, claim and take, and be a great white shark. Don't give an inch. But when you are interacting with others, in a noncompetitive format, such as with neighbors and friends at school and church, be compassionate and kind, be open and share.

Beautiful. Fierce. Compassionate. Tender. Strong leader. Always keep God first in your life and love your family. I'm excited to see you grow and develop. You are an amazing young woman already. I'm proud of you, and I love you.

Love,
Dad

Dass,

You are a creative and beautiful leader.

Your name is Hadassah, after the strong queen who saved her people. She was beautiful, just like you. *Hadassah* means "myrtle flower," a flower that has beautiful, white, star-shaped leaves. Myrtle flowers are symbols for peace and hope. You are full of hope. You have the strength of a queen and would make a great one.

You are also named after your great-great-grandmother, who raised my grandmother Helen, who raised me. I suspect Helen got her tenderness and kindness from her.

You come from a long line of tender and caring women. Great women. Their legacy is passed on to you. I can see them in you. You have sensitivity and tenderness. Your feelings are a gift. Artists can feel and sense things that others cannot. Your great-great-grandmother Nettie was a renowned artist. I suspect she had your vision and sensibilities. You can sometimes feel others' feelings without them saying a word. But sometimes, your feelings are so strong they can overwhelm you.

Your feelings are real, but they are not the only truth or the full story. When big feelings come at me, I allow myself to feel them, then pause and breathe. I've learned it's best not to blurt out an emotional reaction. I pause and then try to speak from a place of peace. Wait for the storm to pass, consider, use your discernment, then act from a place of peace.

Many children make decisions based only on their feelings. (Many adults do this too.) But when you do this, you can be irrational or impulsive or make a choice you later regret. Pay attention to your feelings, but know they are not the only factor in your decisions. Pausing is wise. Consider the situation; consider your response. In most cases, it is best to allow the strongest emotions to simmer before speaking. Don't react. Don't speak in anger or irritation or frustration.

We visited a theme park called Silver Dollar City. We did the log ride, and the train, and Eva got her face painted. We rode the Fire-in-the-Hole roller coaster. You girls talked about how it made your stomachs drop. When you live by your feelings, life can feel like a roller coaster. You never know when you will have good days or bad days, good moments or bad moments. Sometimes you have all of them within seconds of one another. It feels like you are strapped to this spinning, wild, out-of-control thing. Life can feel helpless when we are strapped to the whims of our emotions, whipping around mercilessly while our stomachs drop.

Do your best not to live by your emotions. In the sad or hard times, try drawing or writing. If you can't find the words, try writing poetry. Poetry is basically writing with no rules. A flow of feelings and thoughts. I have found if I can just get those thoughts and feelings out, it helps.

You are fearless. You did your first flip off the balance beam when you were five. No one prompted you or taught you. You just did it. Wow! Our eyes got big, and we all said, "Wait, what just happened?" You had zero fear. This past year in soccer, you chased down the ball and did a slide tackle on a girl who was a foot taller than you. You slid and blocked another goal at the last second. Afterward, Coach Jason said you were player of the game! You play basketball the same way, and you led your team in scoring this year.

You are full of creativity, passion, and curious energy. You see things from a different perspective. Your mind is always looking for some unique angle, something no one else sees. Creative people do this; it's a powerful gift. Creative people have vision. You dance, draw, write, and listen to music this same way, looking for your own unique expression. When you work on the computer, you make designs, write stories, and create art. Your vision, passion, and deep sensitivity are powerful, creative forces.

The creative mind is powerful. At times it can be focused for hours and days on a task; other times it can seem to move in all directions at once. Some of the most creative people I know have messy desks. They have sticky notes, pictures, and little things flung here and there. But I have found, with me, that it is best to have structure. I structure my days where there are consistent time blocks dedicated to certain things. This structure does not come naturally for me. If I structure my day in time blocks and stay consistent, it helps with my creative process.

Wake and pray. Read the verse of the day. Write. Work out. Eat lunch. Rest. Pick you girls up from school. Play. Practice. Eat dinner. Write again and prep for tomorrow. Sleep.

You can make things, do things, and write things that will change the world. Some of the best creatives in the world are women. Many of them are young women. Alyssa is going to design school in New York at age eighteen. Lauren Daigle is in her twenties. Some of the best writers have been women. Maya Angelou. Jane Austen. Mary Oliver. Agatha Christie. Ann Voskamp. Fran Walsh and Philippa Boyens helped write the screenplays for The Lord of the Rings trilogy.

You're a great listener. This skill will help you for the rest of your life. This year, we worked on your basketball game. We practiced every week, reworked your shot, dribbling, defense, and jab step. You listened and learned all of it. Instead of backing up, we worked on the triple-threat position. The next game, you were double-teamed and brought the ball down to your side to create space, then shot over the other players and made it!

Anyone who becomes great at anything must have the humility to listen. You don't need to listen to everyone, though. Everyone has advice. Choose wisely. You only need one or two of the best coaches, mentors, or teachers you can find, and then listen to and learn from them. Pride stands in the way of learning and listening; pride stunts the growth of your destiny.

Remember, please don't take it personally when a coach gives you a correction. I know it feels personal and emotional whenever someone corrects you. It doesn't feel like they approve of you or like you. Good coaches will encourage you and give you things to work on. (There are a lot of bad coaches out there.) If you can listen to good coaches and mentors, and not take offense, you can be far, far better than you could be otherwise.

When you write your first book, many people will give you constructive criticism. Most of my book ideas get rejected. It just comes with the territory. Listen and try to glean wisdom and get better from what they are saying. Keep an open posture. And remember, sometimes coaches (and publishers) are not always right. Don't let them rush you. Don't get a book deal until your book is mostly finished. Hurry often ruins art.

Beautiful. Fearless. Sensitive. Imaginative. Creative leader. Always keep God first in your life and love your family. I'm excited to see you grow and develop. You are an amazing young woman already. I'm proud of you, and I love you.

Love,
Dad

Evangeline,

You are a joyful and beautiful leader.

Your name is Evangeline, which means "the good news of God." You bring so much joy, laughter, and goodness to everyone you meet. You are brimming with love.

You are younger than the other biggies, so we haven't known you as long. But you may have the most to teach us. There's a radiance about you. You shine with bright sparks of purity and light. Things I used to have when I was younger but lost somewhere along the way. Being with you reminds me of these things and makes me long for them and want them back.

Tonight, you were lying on my chest. Your sisters were already asleep. But you were being a floppy fish. My chest was your pond. After flopping on me for a while, you seemed to get a little frustrated and asked, "Daddy? Can you sing me?"

"Of course, sweetheart. What do you want me to sing?"

"Silent Night," you said. "Silent Night" is the perfect song for you. You are full of good news. When I was your age, I lit candles and sang it every Christmas Eve, sitting next to my grandmother at All Souls Church.

And your joy is a superpower. Joy is a deep well of contentment, trust, and happiness that stays. Joy is resilient. Tough. Joy doesn't rise and fall on the changing tides of emotion. You are bursting with it. Even when drama is around you, you smile and keep your joy. And the purest joy comes from God. It will sustain you.

Joy doesn't mean you are never sad or don't have rough days. Joy doesn't pretend. It just means that underneath everything, there is a strong river that cannot be touched. Joyful leaders are often the strongest leaders. Their whole lives are an inspiration.

You care, love, and defend your people. I love seeing you stand up for your sisters. When one sister doesn't do the right thing, you sense it, want to make it right, and say in a loud voice, "Stop!" The other day, I put you in charge. I said, "Okay, Eva, you are in charge." You loved it. The big girls listened to you and respected what you had to say. You did not allow them to argue or fuss or have bad attitudes. You kept the peace. Well done.

Love protects, and you are a strong protector and peacekeeper. You stand up for your sisters and me. You are caring and compassionate too. When someone feels bad, you have loads of care, and you bring gifts, blankets, food, and tenderness. You drop everything to look for whatever we need. When someone is sad, you often draw a picture to cheer them up.

You love giving gifts, and you are a gift.

Gratitude is a rhythm for you. It comes out of your heart naturally. Maybe more than anyone I have ever seen. And if you keep this, your gratitude will protect your peace and joy. You are genuinely thankful for the moment, to be where you are, wherever you are.

You often thank me for things I did weeks and months earlier. You have a great memory, and when you are thankful for something, you feel and speak it. You don't just thank someone in that transactional moment, like, "Here is a cupcake." "Thank you, Daddy." You remember and take it in and are deeply grateful. You wear gratitude like a beautiful raiment.

You want to do right. You are always quick to obey and say, "Yes, Daddy." You love *PAW Patrol;* you love watching Skye, Marshall, and Chase save the day. Sometimes you spend hours saving the day with them. You are a justice fighter. You like sword fighting. You own a few swords. I gave you the Princess Knight sword for Christmas. Sometimes we have tea parties. Sometimes we have sword fights. And I can see you doing great good in the world, bringing your joy and love and light. Whatever you set your heart to do, you will be amazing.

You are fast, and you are fearless. When you were three, you could speed on the scooter almost as fast as a grown-up on a bike! That's fast. You fly down the road on your pink scooter. You love to move.

The other day you rode without training wheels. Three years old is really young to ride a big bike with no training wheels, but you did. It was awesome. And you are good at gymnastics and the balance beam. You are a great jumper and a great dancer. It requires freedom and courage to dance, and you have both.

Sometimes you have vivid dreams. Dreams you remember for weeks. Sometimes God speaks through dreams. Maybe God speaks to you this way too. He gave Joseph a dream, a vision of Joseph's future. He gave Daniel dreams, dreams that helped Daniel see, make good decisions, and lead. Centuries later, an angel appeared to another Joseph in a dream and told him about the Son he was having. Your dreams are powerful. Remember them. Consider them.

Beautiful. Caring. Grateful. Fast and fearless. Justice fighter. Joyful leader. Always keep God first in your life and love your family. I'm excited to see you grow and develop. You are an amazing young woman already. I'm proud of you, and I love you.

Love,
Dad

SAY ALL YOUR OWN UNSPOKEN THINGS

Questions for the Reader

As you read these letters, maybe you've realized that you, too, have words and feelings stranded in your heart. Don't let this moment pass. I encourage you to grab a pen or a keyboard and tell your loved ones all the things you've thought and felt but perhaps have never spoken.

You don't have to be a writer to say all your own unspoken things to your spouse, your children, your parents, your loved ones. In fact, the unpolished words are often the truest. Your own voice—your stories, your thoughts, the way you express yourself in your own unique words—will be a lasting treasure and legacy. The important thing is simply to start.

Below are some questions to help you get started. You can use them as springboards to express your stories, advice, and feelings—or come up with something that is entirely your own! Whether lengthy or short, letters or prose, whatever feels most natural to you, now is the time to capture your stories and memories and say all the things you've always wanted to say.

After you've written and shared your letters, consider sharing some of them with others. With your loved ones' permission, post a few lines on facebook.com/theunspokenthings or reach out to me directly at instagram.com/johnsowers. I hope you are bold and truthful and hold nothing back and say all the unspoken things.

Yours sincerely,

John

You Are Created

1. If writing to your children, what details do you remember about your children's births? How did you feel when they were born? What do you wish you could have said to them on the day each of them was born?

2. What would you say today about your children? About how they were created for relationship? What does that mean to you?

3. If writing to your spouse, parents, or friends, what do you appreciate about the fact that God created them? How do their lives make your life better today?

4. What are your earliest memories with that loved one? What were your first impressions of that person? What are some of the things you first did together? Share your stories.

5. How do you view the Father? Do you confuse him with the older brother, angry and judgmental? Have judgmental people ever pushed you away from God?

Identity and Purpose

1. How would you describe your loved one? In what ways can you encourage your loved one to look past what the world may say about them to see their unchanging identity as a child of God?

2. What do you think your loved one's purpose is? What are they good at? What are their talents? Where do they shine, as if they were made for this?

3. Many people hop from one false identity to the next, searching for meaning and purpose. Share your stories about discovering your own identity and purpose. How can you encourage your loved ones to fulfill their true eternal purposes in their unique gifts and callings?

4. What does it mean to make your life a song? How do we join in the Song?

5. Have you ever started a gratitude journal? How did that go? Do you still journal?

Growing Young

1. How would you describe your loved ones' sense of wonder, imagination, and freedom? In what ways can you encourage your loved ones to keep a sense of wonder, even as they grow older? Do you still dream and imagine, or have you lost something there?

2. Why do you think people try to crush our dreams or want us to have a more realistic perspective? If this has happened to you, share your story. How should your loved ones respond to dream crushers?

3. What is something (on the inside) you want to recover that you have lost?

4. How has courage shown up in your story? Write down a time you were brave.

5. How does the world define *beautiful*? Have you seen this affect you? How do you define *beautiful*?

Becoming

1. As you observe your loved ones day by day, who are they becoming? What kinds of seeds are they planting in their hearts and lives?

2. In what ways can you encourage your loved ones to make wise choices? Share your stories of wise choices (or not-so-wise choices) to illustrate the importance of seeking God's wisdom in our daily lives. What are some of your best decisions? How do our daily decisions shape us?

3. Why do you think people try to push you into becoming something other than your design? What can you say to encourage your loved ones to stay true to themselves through the years?

4. What are your normals? Are you a reflection or reaction to your parents? What things did you bring from your childhood into adulthood? What things would you want to let go?

5. Have you ever heard a whisper from God in your heart? How did you respond? How did it change your life?

6. Have you ever walked in the Spirit? How do you do this? What is it like? How and when do you connect with God?

Developing Character

1. What are some positive character traits you have observed in your loved ones? Be specific.

2. Write down a time you have seen humility help, repair, and restore a relationship.

3. Write down a time you have seen pride destroy a relationship.

4. How has kindness impacted you? Can you remember a moment where kindness transformed you or another person?

5. What character traits would you like your loved ones to continue to develop? Share your stories about how people with those character traits (such as kindness, gratitude, and so on) have positively influenced your life.

6. Sometimes we make mistakes or wrong choices and believe we are unworthy. Remind your loved ones of their true worth, no matter what circumstances they may encounter in life.

Friends and Relationships

1. What makes a good friend? Share some of your stories of people who have been good friends to you. What do you appreciate about your friends, such as showing kindness, listening to you, and encouraging you?

2. How can you be a good friend to others? What does it mean to value others above yourself? What are some observations and stories about friendship you'd like to share?

3. Are you a friend initiator, or do you wait for others to come to you? Do you seek to encourage others?

4. What are your boundaries in friendships and relationships? Have you ever had to enforce them? If so, what happened?

5. Why is it so important to choose your friends and relationships wisely? Have you ever given in to peer pressure? Encourage your loved ones to set boundaries and guard their hearts as they connect with others.

6. Are you part of a spiritual family? What is that like? Who is in your spiritual family, and what do you love most about it? How does your spiritual family influence you? Do you pray with others?

Finding and Being in Love

1. What advice can you share with your loved ones about finding love? Share some of your stories of young love or romantic love, being sure to speak of your former partners in an honoring way.

2. In what ways could your loved ones' upbringings and parents influence their future relationships? Share what you'd encourage them to imitate and what you'd like them not to repeat.

3. What are your love languages? What are the love languages of your spouse, friends, children?

4. How would you describe a healthy, thriving, God-honoring marriage relationship? Share your thoughts and experiences on choosing (and being) a good spouse, waiting on God, sex and purity, intimacy, honesty, and faithfulness.

5. Have you seen the effects of the Golden Cloud in your life, or have you observed people make decisions based on their feelings? If so, describe what happened.

6. What is the difference between face-to-face intimacy and side-by-side intimacy? Have you ever had a relationship with both postures?

Dreams and Legacy

1. What dreams do you have for yourself? For your loved ones? What are some of your loved ones' dreams? What dreams have you given up on?

2. Why is it important to start making legacy choices from an early age, to live into your dreams now instead of waiting for "someday"? Share your stories of how you followed (or didn't follow) a dream and how that affected your life.

3. Have you ever faced resistance or defeats? How did you respond?

4. In what ways can you encourage your loved ones to live their lives for the good? How might you inspire them to fulfill their dreams and leave a legacy of faithfulness for their own children and grandchildren someday?

ACKNOWLEDGMENTS

Thank you, God, for loving me and giving me grace in Jesus, for life and breath and forgiveness when I don't deserve it and never have.

To my daughters, Rosie, Dass, and Evangeline, I love you with my whole heart. There are many more things I would say to you if I had more time and books did not have to be finished by such and such date and turned in to editors and people with red pens. And I have more letters to write, things to say about work, money, service, and giving your time to worthy causes. I have things to say about making sure you don't run yourselves into the ground and making sure you rest, exercise, eat right, and take care of your teeth, skin, and bodies. But these things will have to wait for another time. I hope this book encourages and helps you in your lives, for your whole lives. I hope you pass it down to your children and to their children too. I hope I live and model the words in this book, and where I do not, where I fall short, I hope you can give me grace and see the best in me.

No book happens alone. There are many involved friends, editors, designers, and a whole host of other people. I am so grateful to write this book with HarperCollins, Thomas Nelson, and the W Publishing team. I am grateful to have the opportunity to write and put words out into the world. To Don, thank you for encouraging and mentoring me and being a constant friend, even through the hard times. Thank you for giving me the opportunity to publish this book and for being one of the best men I know. Thank you to Damon, Kyle, Jen, Meaghan, Whitney, and the rest of those who have worked hard, prayed, Zoom-called, and discussed and plotted with me. Thank you for letting me inflict my writing on you. Thanks for believing in me and this book and for making me a better writer.

To my mom and grandmother for raising me and teaching me to love books, writing, words, and stories. Thank you for your legacy, how you showed up for me and loved me. Your legacy is the inspiration for my life and this book. I hope to do and be the things you taught me to do and be. I'm so grateful for you both and how you poured your lives out for me. You never wavered, you never flinched, you loved me from my first breath until you left. Thank you, thank you, thank you.

To Daniella, thank you for loving and believing in me and praying these words into existence. This book would not be here if not for you. Bill, thanks for what you said about me at Mom's funeral. I'll never forget that. Addison. Zack. Alyssa. Jodie. Dad. Chris. Kari. Jim. Gloria. Carla. Braden. Brooklyn. Aubrey. Thank you.

To my friends who spoke into my life and showed up during the hard times. You guys worked overtime the past few years, and I could not make it without you. Ed, thank you for being one of the best men I know. I am honored and privileged to call you friend. I love you and Gretchen. I'm so grateful for so many of my friends who have listened to me, cried with me, called me, texted me, and encouraged me. Devo, Ben and Ang, Nick and Krysta, Angela, Diane, Brother Phelps, David, Cameron, Gail, Duke and Caroline, Mark, Mike, Charlie, Don, Bob, Kurt, Jim, Clay, Eric, Matt, Bruce, Brandon and Jen, Roy, Liz, Josh, Kim, Zack, Burris, Jon, Sonny, LPG, Keith, Stacy,

Lauri, Scott, Blair, Barb and Dustin, Chad and Myquillyn, Leah, Matt, Tommy, Timothy, Griffin.

To the coffee shops that let me sit in your place, drink your coffee for long hours, and write this book. Thanks for not kicking me out when I sat in the corner with sunglasses on and looked like some kind of creeper. Sharon at Honey Pies in Little Rock, I will never forget what you did for my mom. And you have the best banana pudding ever. Thank you to the Workshop in Ozark and Architect Coffee Co. and Springtown Coffee Co. in Springfield.

To the musicians and artists who inspire me every day with your words, music, and songs; I listened to many of you during this writing. Sleeping at Last. U2. Propaganda. John Mark McMillan and Kim Walker-Smith. Dermot Kennedy. Boon. Jon Shirley. Charlie Hall. Josh Garrels. David Gray. And many others.

And to you, reading this book. Thank you. I'd love to meet you someday. I hope to come to your town, maybe a local bookstore or Barnes and Noble. You can find me on Instagram at johnsowers, instagram.com/johnsowers. Comment and I'll say hello.

I hope this book inspires you and unlocks some things in your heart too.

Thanks again for reading. For real.

NOTES

The Unspoken Things

xii   **Adam and Eve, who fell:** Genesis 3:7.

Chapter 1: Created

4   **"You created my inmost being":** Psalm 139:13, 15–16.

5   **[You were] created through him and for him:** Colossians 1:16.

Chapter 2: With

10   **The Bible says his name is Immanuel:** Matthew 1:23.

10   **He created the universe by speaking it into being:** Psalm 33:9.

Chapter 3: Dad

14   **A story of a dad who had two sons:** Luke 15:11–24, author's paraphrase.

14   **"I am no longer worthy to be called your son":** Luke 15:19, 21, ESV.

15   **"I am the prodigal son":** Henri Nouwen, *The Return of the Prodigal Son* (New York: Doubleday, 1992; New York: Image Books, 1994), 43.

15   **"The victorious limp":** Brennan Manning, *The Ragamuffin Gospel* (Colorado Springs: Multnomah Books, 2005), 178.

Chapter 4: Home

18 **A second part to the story:** Luke 15:25–31, author's paraphrase.

20 **"My Father's house has many rooms":** John 14:2.

Chapter 5: Life

27 **There is nothing more beautiful than death:** Walt Whitman, "Starting from Paumanok," in *Walt Whitman: The Complete Poems*, ed. Francis Murphy (1975; repr., London: Penguin Books, 2004), 57, st. 12, line 169.

28 **"I am the resurrection and the life":** John 11:25–26 ESV.

28 **"At the death of death":** "Death of Death" featuring Charlie Hall, Spotify, track 15 on Passion, *Passion: Let the Future Begin* (Deluxe Edition), Sparrow Records, 2013.

Chapter 6: Song

30 **God finally answered Job:** Job 38:4, 7 NLT.

30 **The "invisible piper":** Albert Einstein, quoted in Ronald W. Clark, *Einstein: The Life and Times* (New York: Avon Books, 1972; repr., 2001), 422.

30 **God has put eternity in the heart:** Ecclesiastes 3:11, author's paraphrase.

31 **He heard a song:** Mark Wheeler, "Signal Discovery?," *Smithsonian*, March 2004, https://www.smithsonianmag.com/science-nature/signal-discovery-104663195/.

31 **Many people with dementia:** Ronald Devere, "Music and Dementia: An Overview," *Practical Neurology*, June 2017, https://practicalneurology.com/articles/2017-june/music-and-dementia-an-overview.

31 **A special kind of neutron star:** Macro Tavani et al., "An X-ray Burst from a Magnetar Enlightening the Mechanism of Fast Radio Bursts," *Nature Astronomy* 5 (February 2021): 401–7, https://doi.org/10.1038/s41550-020-01276-x.

32 **"God lives in the praises of his people":** Psalm 22:3, author's paraphrase.

32   **"Be filled with the spirit":** Ephesians 5:18–19.

33   **Our lives are stories:** Donald Miller, *A Million Miles in a Thousand Years: What I Learned While Editing My Life* (Nashville: Thomas Nelson, 2009).

33   **"Set your hearts on things above":** Colossians 3:1–2.

34   **"Those who sow with tears":** Psalm 126:5.

Chapter 7: Thankful

36   **"No disaster, no storm, no cancellation":** Ann Voskamp, "A Story: How One Unlikely Man Stopped the Stealing of Thanksgiving," *(in)courage* (blog), November 17, 2015, https://www.incourage.me/2015/11/a-story-how-one-unlikely-man-stopped-the-stealing-of-thanksgiving.html.

37   **"Complaints have no magic":** Cleo Wade, *Heart Talk: Poetic Wisdom for a Better Life* (New York: Atria 3, 2018), 106.

38   **Gratitude rewires our brains:** Joshua Brown and Joel Wong, "How Gratitude Changes You and Your Brain," *Greater Good* Magazine, June 6, 2017, https://greatergood.berkeley.edu/article/item/how_gratitude_changes_you_and_your_brain.

38   **She was the Giving Tree:** Shel Silverstein, *The Giving Tree* (New York: Harper & Row, 1964).

Chapter 8: Wonder

44   **"The most beautiful thing":** Albert Einstein et al., *Living Philosophies* (New York: Simon and Schuster, 1931), 6.

44   **"The universe is full of magical things":** Eden Phillpotts, *A Shadow Passes* (London: Cecil Palmer & Hayward, 1918), 19.

44   **"To see a world in a grain of sand":** William Blake, "Auguries of Innocence," in *The Pickering Manuscript* (Whitefish, MT: Kessinger Publishing, 2004), 15.

Chapter 9: Brave

50   **"We cannot be proud of the violence":** Georgia Dortch and Jane Emery, "The Price We Pay," *Tiger*, September 19, 1957, http://jackiewhiting.net/collab/CivRts/Tiger.htm.

51   **"When that white driver":** Donnie Williams and Wayne Greenhaw, *The Thunder of Angels: The Montgomery Bus Boycott and the People Who Broke the Back of Jim Crow* (Chicago: Lawrence Hill Books, 1953), 48.

51   **"Courage doesn't always roar":** Mary Anne Radmacher, *Courage Doesn't Always Roar* (San Francisco: Conari Press, 2009).

52   **"Sophie did not waiver":** Sophie Scholl (trial in Munich, Germany, February 22, 1943), in Whitney Milam, "Sophie Scholl: The German Student Who Led an Anti-Nazi Resistance Movement," Amy Poehler's Smart Girls, April 2, 2017, https://amysmartgirls.com/sophie-scholl-the-german-student-who-led-an-anti-nazi-resistance-movement-ef4c8d2f4d96.

Chapter 10: Beautiful

55   **God made man and woman:** Genesis 1:27.

55   **We are . . . changed from glory to glory:** 2 Corinthians 3:18.

55   **The truth of Jesus:** John 16:33.

56   **"The most beautiful people we have known":** Elisabeth Kübler-Ross, ed., *Death: The Final Stage of Growth* (1975; repr., New York: Touchstone, 1986), 96.

56   **"It doesn't have to be perfect":** Myquillyn Smith, *The Nesting Place: It Doesn't Have to Be Perfect to Be Beautiful* (Grand Rapids: Zondervan, 2014).

Chapter 11: Seeds

60   **"Every moment and every event":** Thomas Merton, *New Seeds of Contemplation* (1972; repr., New York: New Directions, 2007), 14.

61   **"A word that describes the default 'me'":** Gordon MacDonald, *A Resilient Life: You Can Move Ahead No Matter What* (Nashville: Thomas Nelson, 2004), 61–62.

61   **"The wisdom that comes from heaven":** James 3:17.

63   **"Whatever is true":** Philippians 4:8.

Chapter 12: Fingerprints

68 **"I never exactly made a book":** C. S. Lewis Institute–Chicago, Facebook, November 30, 2013, https://www.facebook.com /CSLIChicago/posts/187558791435121.

Chapter 13: Normals

70 **"No man is an island, entire of itself":** John Donne, *Devotions upon Emergent Occasions*, in Henry Alford, ed., *The Works of John Donne* (London: John W. Parker, 1839), 3:575.

71 **"Walk with the wise":** Proverbs 13:20.

Chapter 14: Whispers

73 **"His mercies are new every morning":** Lamentations 3:23, author's paraphrase.

73 **"There was evening":** Genesis 1:5.

73 **"On the seventh day":** Genesis 2:2.

73 **The lifespan for the average American:** Rabah Kamal, "How Does U.S. Life Expectancy Compare to Other Countries?," Health System Tracker, December 23, 2019, https://www.healthsystemtracker.org /chart-collection/u-s-life-expectancy-compare-countries/#item -start.

74 **Billy mailed me a book:** Billy Graham, *Peace with God: The Secret of Happiness* (1953; repr., Nashville: Thomas Nelson, 2017).

75 **"God whispers to those who trust him":** Psalm 25:14, author's paraphrase.

75 **There was a young boy named Samuel:** 1 Samuel 3.

75 **God told Elijah that he was not alone:** 1 Kings 19:1–18.

75 **Sometimes we lose our sense of sight:** Acts 9:9.

Chapter 15: Filled

80 **"In him we live and move and have our being":** Acts 17:28.

82 **"Walking in the Spirit is a rhythm":** Stacy Dollar, personal communication to author, December 2020.

82   **Good things are formed in my heart:** Galatians 5:22–23.

82   **Paul shared his inner conflict:** Romans 7:15, 19.

83   **"Jesus went to a solitary place":** Mark 1:35, author's paraphrase.

83   **"It comes the very moment":** C. S. Lewis, *Mere Christianity* (New York: HarperCollins, 2001), 198.

Chapter 16: Humble

88   **Edited photos are a new form of torture:** Alex Williams, "The Agony of Instagram," *New York Times*, December 13, 2013, https://www.nytimes.com/2013/12/15/fashion/instagram.html.

91   **"Jesus, remember me":** Luke 23:42.

91   **"God, have mercy on me":** Luke 18:13.

91   **"Humility comes before honor":** Proverbs 18:12.

Chapter 17: Kind

96   **"No kind action ever stopped with itself":** Frederick William Faber, *Spiritual Conferences* (Baltimore: John Murphy, 1859), 30.

Chapter 18: Enough

97   **Put it in a song:** Ryan O'Neal, "Four," Sleeping at Last (website), April 13, 2018, http://www.sleepingatlast.com/blog/2017/11/17/three-s82w5.

100   **"There is no fear in love":** 1 John 4:18.

Chapter 19: Queen

104   **"Do not think that because":** Esther 4:13–14.

105   **"When this is done, I will go to the king":** Esther 4:16.

Chapter 20: Words

108   **"A good man brings good things":** Luke 6:45.

109   **"A bit in the mouth of a horse":** James 3:3–6 MSG.

Chapter 22: Boundaries

120   **"Boundaries define us":** Henry Cloud and John Townsend, *Boundaries, Participants's Guide* (Grand Rapids: Zondervan, 1999), 10–18.

Chapter 23: Spiritual Family

126 **The chapter talks about:** Isaiah 61:3–4.

127 **Jesus quoted the first part of this chapter:** Luke 4:18.

128 **"We had to play it honest":** Duke Revard, personal correspondence with author, March 2021.

Chapter 24: Love as Being

132 **Jesus told a story about a man:** Luke 10:25–37, author's paraphrase.

132 **You can read this story in his book:** Bob Goff, *Everybody Always: Becoming Love in a World Full of Setbacks and Difficult People* (Nashville: Nelson Books, 2018).

133 **"There's no school to learn how to love":** Goff, *Everybody Always*, 19–20.

134 **"Love is patient":** 1 Corinthians 13:4–8.

135 **"We'll become in our lives":** Goff, *Everybody Always*, 4.

Chapter 25: Love as Knowing

138 **The Latin word for *infatuation*:** *Merriam-Webster*, s.v. "fatuous," accessed May 3, 2021, https://www.merriam-webster.com /dictionary/fatuous.

139 **She dreams about romance:** Kristen Bell and Idina Menzel, vocalists, "For the First Time in Forever," by Kristen Anderson-Lopez and Robert Lopez, Spotify, track 3 on *Frozen* (Original Motion Picture Soundtrack), Walt Disney Records, 2013.

139 **They "conceal, don't feel":** Idina Menzel, vocalist, "Let It Go," by Kristen Anderson-Lopez and Robert Lopez, Spotify, track 5 on *Frozen* (Original Motion Picture Soundtrack), Walt Disney Records, 2013.

140 **"To love at all is to be vulnerable":** C. S. Lewis, *The Four Loves* (1960; repr., New York: Harcourt Brace, 1991), 121.

140 **Before, they walked with God:** Genesis 3:8.

Chapter 26: Romantic Love

142 **It is "a process":** Adrienne Rich, "Women and Honor: Some Notes on Lying (1975)," in *On Lies, Secrets, and Silence: Selected Prose, 1996–1978* (New York: W. W. Norton, 1979), 188.

143 **Two complete strangers could love each other:** Arthur Aron et al., "The Experimental Generation of Interpersonal Closeness: A Procedure and Some Preliminary Findings," *Personality and Social Psychology Bulletin* 23, no. 4 (Apr l 1997): 363–77, https://journals .sagepub.com/doi/10.1177/0146167297234003.

144 **"Need-love says":** C. S. Lewis, *The Four Loves* (1960; repr., New York: Harcourt Brace, 1991), 17.

144 **One book that has taught me:** Gary Chapman, *The 5 Love Languages: The Secret to Love That Lasts* (1992; repr., Chicago: Northfield, 2015).

Chapter 27: The Golden Cloud

149 **"The love partner becomes the divine ideal":** Ernest Becker, *The Denial of Death* (1973; repr., New York: Free Press Paperbacks, 1997), 160, 167.

150 **"It is more blessed to give than to receive":** Acts 20:35.

150 **"The one principle of hell is-'I am my own'":** George MacDonald, *Unspoken Sermons* (New York: Cosimo, 2007), 332.

Chapter 28: Pursuit and Peace

152 **"I will find out where she has gone":** William Butler Yeats, "The Song of Wandering Aengus," in *The Wind among the Reeds* (London: Elkin Mathews, 1899), 16.

153 **"Beautiful things don't ask for attention":** *The Secret Life of Walter Mitty*, directed by Ben Stiller (2013; Los Angeles: 20th Century Fox Home Entertainment, 2014), DVD.

156 **"Do not be anxious about anything":** Philippians 4:6–7.

Chapter 29: Dreams

159 **0.0296% of Little League baseball players:** "What Are the Chances a Little League Baseball Player Gets to the Major Leagues Someday?," Spreadsheet Solving, accessed May 4, 2021, https://spreadsheetsolving.com/little-league/.

161 **"Fear is going to be a player in your life":** Jim Carrey, "Choose Love, and Don't Ever Let Fear Turn You against Your Playful Heart" (commencement address, Maharishi University of Management, Fairfield, Iowa, May 24, 2014), 10:12, https://www.youtube.com/watch?v=V80-gPkpH6M&t=582s&ab_channel=MaharishiInternationalUniversity.

162 **A boy named Joseph dreamed:** Genesis 37:5–11; 42:6; 43:26, 28.

162 **[Joseph] grew and the Lord was with him:** Genesis 39:2, 23.

Chapter 30: Dedication

168 **"I dreamed about playing guitar":** Ed Eason, personal communication with author, September 2020.

168 **The parable of the talents:** Matthew 25:14–30, ESV.

Chapter 31: Dedication (Tips)

174 **"It is not the critic who counts":** Theodore Roosevelt, "Citizenship in a Republic" (speech, Sorbonne, Paris, France, April 23, 1910), https://www.leadershipnow.com/tr-citizenship.html.

175 **"A wise man is impressed by a rebuke":** Proverbs 17:10, author's paraphrase.

176 **"Hold yourself responsible":** Henry Ward Beecher, "Ward Beecher's Advice to His Son," *Railway Signal 9*, no. 7 (July 1891): 149.

Chapter 32: Resistance

178 **"When I was young, I switched from swimming to water polo":** Rosanna Tomiuk, personal communication with author, November 2020.

179 **What Thoreau called "quiet desperation":** Henry David Thoreau, *Walden: or, Life in the Woods* (New York: Houghton, Mifflin, 1899), 15.

179 **"Everybody goes through disappointments":** Michael Jordan, interview on *The Tonight Show with Jay Leno*, aired September 16, 1997, on NBC.

180 **"For such a time as this":** Esther 4:14.

Chapter 33: Time

184 **We know that the angels shout:** Luke 15:10, author's paraphrase.

184 **We know there will be singing in heaven:** Revelation 14:3; 15:3.

185 **Our mortal lives are like vapor:** James 4:14.

186 **"Love God":** Bob Goff, Twitter post, December 14, 2013, https://twitter.com/bobgoff/status/411870042683236353?s=20.

186 **"The things you used to own":** Chuck Palahniuk, *Fight Club* (New York: W. W. Norton, 2005), 44.

187 **"When you are old and grey and full of sleep":** William Butler Yeats, "When You Are Old," *The Collected Poems of W. B. Yeats* (Ware, England: Wordsworth Editions, 1994), 32.

ABOUT THE AUTHOR

John Sowers is a published author, speaker, and cofounder of the Mentoring Project with Donald Miller. John's work and writings have been featured by Fox News, CNN, MSNBC, ESPN, Maria Shriver, Oprah Radio, the *Oregonian*, the *Oklahoman*, and others. John also received President Obama's Champion of Change award at the White House.

Before launching the Mentoring Project, he was the multi-language director for the Billy Graham Evangelistic Association, leading the most diverse outreaches in Billy Graham history, in Los Angeles and New York. He also served with the Billy Graham Rapid Response Team, helped victims of Hurricane Katrina, and spoke in Billy Graham prison outreaches. Before his time with Billy Graham, John directed a homeless shelter, where he fed, clothed, sang, and ate with the homeless every night.

John received his master of divinity from Trinity Evangelical Divinity School and his doctorate from Gordon-Conwell Theological Seminary. He is the author of *Fatherless Generation: Redeeming the Story* and *The Heroic Path: In Search of the Masculine Heart* and has written articles for *Relevant* magazine, *Wilderness*, and other publications. But his favorite accomplishment is being a dad to his daughters, Rosie, Dass, and Eva. John lives in a cabin near Ozark, Missouri.